AN ANGEL KISSED BY GOD

AN ANGEL KISSED BY GOD

An Autism Recovery Story

Judy Ann

To order additional copies of this book, contact:
Xlibris Corporation
1-888-795-4274
www.Xlibris.com
Orders@Xlibris.com
37980

Contents

This book is dedicated to my father, who was the one who taught me what true faith is. To my Mom, who always believed the best in me, and encouraged me more than anyone else to tell this story. To my older children, I could never have seen this reality without your support. To Kevin, who helped me in my endeavor to be understood. I thank you God, that You were with me every step of the way, and for trusting and believing in me enough to entrust me with one of your little angels.

Introduction

I am writing this story to tell you about our lives and my experiences with raising a child diagnosed with Autism. With this story, I hope to give guidance and hope to others going through a similar situation. Having a child that has been diagnosed with any type of illness or disability is heartbreaking to the parents. With a diagnosis of autism, one certainly feels helpless. There are a lot of books that offer information on the subject of Autism. Most of the books I have read made me feel even more depressed and more powerless in my situation. My purpose in writing this book is to share hope with other people. My experiences have truly increased my faith in God. Without God I don't know how I would have ever survived. I hope when you read this book it will show you how to apply faith in God to your situation.

1

THE BEGINNING

The beginning of this story starts way before the moment of conception. I had recently remarried. My new husband and I desperately wanted a child of our own to share together. I had two older children from a previous marriage. After getting married my husband and I discussed my having a tubal ligation reversal surgery in order for us to have a child. This is considered to be an elective surgery and most insurance companies do not cover the procedure. We prayed about our wanting a child of our own, and asked God to make a way for us to have one if it was in His will for us.

My husband was active duty in the military. One day, while my husband was at work, he overheard some women talking about military hospitals that were performing tubal ligation reversal surgeries. My husband asked them a few questions to get more information. He called me and was so excited; we felt this was an answer to our many prayers. He told me he had received information and phone numbers of doctors that were doing reversal surgeries. I called and requested an information packet. I was told to fill it out and return it. Once the packet was returned, we would then go on a waiting list. We could be on that list for six months to two years. We began praying that if this was God's will for us that He would open the door for me to have the surgery. I received the packet, filled out all of the information, and returned the packet in April. A few weeks later, we were notified to attend an orientation. They had a very strict criterion for qualifying for the surgery. I was given an appointment date for my first doctor visit. We had to travel six hours one-way to make these appointments. We were given several doctor appointments, and several tests were done on my husband and me. We had to pass all of these tests, before I was given a surgery date. I had my tubal ligation reversal surgery in September. This was only five months after returning the information packet. We both felt that our prayers were being answered and God was making a way.

My surgery was successful, I was told I would have about a 75% success rate of getting pregnant within the first six months and the percentage would go down from there and the risk of a tubal pregnancy would become higher. We both thanked God that He had brought us through this ordeal with no problems. We were so excited.

Soon after my surgery my father became very ill and was hospitalized. This was a very difficult time for us. After being in a hospital for some time, my father died. Nine days later, I found out I was pregnant. Due to the overwhelming stress during this time, I miscarried within two weeks. We were heartbroken. It was very difficult to grieve over the death of my father, as well as a miscarriage. God gave me a dream. I had experienced 4 miscarriages up to this point in my life. I had a dream that I was sitting on the lower part of a big hill; it was covered with beautiful green grass. I looked up toward the top of the hill, and saw my father standing there. He was holding hands with two little girls. Two other little girls were holding onto their hands. They stopped at the top of the hill and then they let go of my father's hands. The girls ran toward me calling mommy, mommy. They were different sizes and different ages. They were each dressed in frilly dresses and shiny shoes. Each had long curled hair of different shades of brown to blond. They ran to me and we embraced. They each sat close to me and I touched them, hugged, and kissed them. We talked for a while about how beautiful heaven was and then my father appeared at the top of the hill again. The girls and I hugged and kissed again; then they ran to my father. When they reached him he turned, smiled, and waved to me. Then they all took hands and walked over the hill and out of sight. This dream gave me great peace and I was able to release my grief and put it into God's hands. I felt this dream was to give my mind peace that my four little girls were in heaven with my dad.

The sixth month point came and went. We were afraid that our time was running out. We still continued on our quest to achieve conception. We continued to pray and although it was hard to wait, we knew the pregnancy would come in God's time.

2

TRYING TO KEEP THE FAITH

In May I got pregnant again. This time when I took the pregnancy test I already knew I was pregnant. I knew in my heart that I was carrying a boy. We had already picked his name. He would be given a name that means Priceless Gift from God. My pregnancy continued with little or no problems. My husband retired from the Navy. We moved from California to Nevada. There was only a very small hospital in the town where we lived and they only delivered babies if it was an emergency. I had to travel 1 1/2 hours one-way to see the doctors or visit the hospital where my son would be delivered. Everything progressed normally until my eighth month.

I was scheduled for a complete ultrasound. I was in a great mood, talking and laughing with the technician doing the test. She assured me that in fact I was carrying a boy. I soon noticed that she kept repeatedly going over the same spot on my stomach and taking measurements. She got up and said that she needed to go get someone and abruptly left the room. I thought that this was really strange. My heart began to beat faster. Both technicians came back into the room and continued to look at the screen, they whispered to each other and one of the technicians left the room again. I asked the technician if everything was OK but she did not answer me. Then the other girl and two doctors entered the room. Both doctors were looking at the screen and shaking their heads. At this point I begin to lose it. I am crying and hysterically asking someone please tell me what is going on, what do you see? One of the doctors finally answers me. He says it appears by the ultrasound that your son has a mass in his head. I am totally hysterical at this point. I asked him to please explain what he means by a mass? One of the doctors looks at me and says it is probably a brain tumor. A brain tumor, did you say a brain tumor? My heart sank to my stomach and my stomach leaked out of my feet. I was shaken. I was in shock. I felt totally helpless. My first reaction was, OH GOD please don't take this baby from me. My mind is reeling. What do we do now? Do they take the baby? Can the baby survive in me for another month? God where are you?

The doctors decided I would need to come into the hospital twice a week for ultrasounds and fetal monitoring. If at any time they felt the baby was in danger, they would take him. I made the three hour round trip to the medical facility twice a week for the next four weeks. I carried this baby and rubbed my stomach and cried out to God for hours every day. I called everyone I knew and asked them to pray. I went into labor on my due date.

I went to the hospital the following morning with labor pains eight minutes apart. When I got to the hospital the nurse checked me and said I was only dilated 2 centimeters' and the baby was still too high so she suggested I go back home, and try to get as much rest as possible. I returned home and tried to rest as much as I could through the day, even though my contractions continued to get harder. At 7:00 p.m. the contractions were now five minutes apart, so we went back to the hospital. (For all of you women out there that have had a child, you know the last thing you want to do when you are having contractions at five minutes apart is to ride in a car for more than one minute). We head out for another 1 1/2 hour ride back to the hospital. When we arrived the nurse checked me again, I was now dilated 6 to 7 centimeters. Within one hour, I was at 9 centimeters' and my water bag broke. I am told that the baby is still too high. The nurse suggested I do an epidural, which I had not used for either of my other two deliveries, but I agree. Then the nurse tells me that my contractions are not hard enough so she gives me some medication to make them stronger. Thank goodness I am feeling no pain. We continue to wait. The baby is still too high, and didn't seem to be moving down at all, despite all of our efforts. By midnight, the baby is still too high, I'm starting to swell and we are still making no progress. After 36 hours of labor they decided to take him by C-section. When the doctor informed me of this, I was upset. I had not prepared myself mentally to have surgery. It was hard to understand why I could not deliver him naturally like I had my other children. I was sort of in shock. I had an adverse reaction to some of the medication they gave me during the delivery and my body began to shake uncontrollably. I remember getting a very brief glimpse of my bundle of joy as they rushed him off to the nursery. I was scared, and my husband stayed by my side until they settled me back in my room. My husband was able to go and bond with our new baby and feed him, but I was not even able to hold him for twelve hours; I was still too groggy from all the medication.

3

OUR CHILD IS BORN

Upon the arrival of our son, he seemed to be perfect in every way. I began to weep and thank God just knowing that He had healed my son. I did not look forward to the time when they came and took this precious little miracle from my arms to do some tests. They took him for the first test. When they brought him back he was freshly bathed. They informed us that the ultrasound they tried to do on his head was unsuccessful. They would have to do a CT scan the following day. I just kept thanking God for healing my son. The following day they took him to do a CT scan. When they returned him, they would not tell us anything. They told us we would have to wait and the pediatrician would come in and discuss the tests with us. The hours dragged by. Finally, she came in. We had never met her before. She explained that the test showed no brain tumor at all. I could have danced around the room. But! Oh I don't like that word at all. As she could not explain what had happened to the tumor, she said, "The test did show something else". There was still another problem. She showed us pictures of his skull from the CT scan and went on to explain. "Normally when a child is born their skull is in several pieces, and there is an opening or what is called the soft spot in the center of the top of the head" she explained. "These pieces of skull overlap during the delivery to allow the baby's head to fit down into the birth canal". She continued, "The pieces of his skull were joined or fused together and this was why he could not come down into the birth canal". She informed us, "She would need to refer him to a specialist, and he would have to have surgery to separate the pieces". All I could do was cry. I was in shock. My faith was shaken. I had prayed for so many hours upon hours for his healing. God, why didn't you answer my prayers?

We made an appointment with the neurosurgeon. His surgery was scheduled to take place when he was five weeks old. The neurosurgeon tried to explain the procedure to us. "The surgery would consist of separating and cutting some of the pieces of his skull out". "The surgery was expected to take about 1 ½ hours". She tried to reassure us that she had done surgery on even smaller babies then him and he would be in good hands. Although she told us he was not suffering any pain, the last week or two prior to the surgery he cried almost constantly. We still had everyone we knew praying for him. It was almost more than I could bear at times. We waited those few weeks and I continued to cry out to God. I still prayed that if he had to go through the surgery that God would guide her hands, and that he would recover fully.

The surgery date finally arrived. It was so hard to put him in the arms of the nurse that morning, knowing there was a risk we would never see him alive again. When the nurse took him, I turned my back and walked toward the door but my husband watched them take him through the door to the surgery room. He even went and looked into the window, which was something I could not have done. He watched them strip him down; he was lying on the bed screaming and he was scared. He said, "He felt that he had betrayed his son because he was turning him over to these people and they were going to hurt him and there was nothing he could do to keep that from happening to his son". It broke my husband's heart. I think he wanted to just take him home or to make this all go away just as much as I did.

There were many risks involved with this type of surgery. Our son could die, be paralyzed, or even have brain damage. We waited for three hours praying and crying as each moment passed. I cried out to God, "Please let everything go Ok, please don't take my baby from me". We knew it was taking longer than expected. That was the longest three hours of my life.

When they finally took him to ICU they had to stabilize him before they would even let me go in. When I finally was allowed to go in, I could not believe my eyes. He was in a small bed with nothing on but a diaper. His head was already beginning to swell. The incision started at his forehead and went to the hairline on the back of his head. There were bruises on his face where they had taped his eyes shut and put his head in a vise during the surgery. I learned later after watching this procedure being done on a cable show, they also give them a drug that paralyzes them before this type of surgery is done. He was hooked up to machines and monitors that kept sounding alarms every few moments. They worked over him constantly for three hours. All I wanted to do was close my eyes and make it all go away. I wanted to pick him up and take him home and everything would be normal. This was not just a bad dream, this was real. I stayed at his side with only a few moments of sleep at a time for the next three days. There was one chair in his room. No one was allowed to sleep in his room. In order to sleep you had to leave the ICU unit and go down the hall to a waiting room. There were two small couches with rod arms. You were not given a pillow or a blanket for comfort. We were asked to leave his room for one hour in the morning and one hour in the evening while they changed shifts. I left the hospital that first night and took my mother and daughter back to our home. My husband stayed with Anthony while I was gone those three hours. The nurses told him they may not let me come back on to the ward when I returned; they had some very strict rules. My husband told them there was no way they would keep me out. They did not make us leave the room the first night. We left his room the following morning to get some breakfast. When we returned, he was screaming and no one was in his room. After that, I never left his room when they changed shifts. That was one rule I did not intend to follow. He was high risk for sleep apnea or could possibly stop breathing. It would sometimes take a nurse up to 30 minutes to respond to one of his alarms. I was going to make sure they didn't let my baby die. They gave us instructions that any time they experienced a code on the floor we would be asked to leave the ward. I told the nurses if they had a code on the floor I would not leave my son's room. I told them I wouldn't leave his side because all of the nurses and doctors would be with the patient experiencing the code, in fact it would be to their benefit for me to care for my own son if this situation happened.

The next few days were very difficult. His whole body swelled from the amount of fluid they had given him to raise his blood pressure. His little body retained the fluid and he went from 10 pounds to 30 pounds.

There was one very strange thing that occurred. Anthony would never use a pacifier at home, but during this time in the hospital he kept the pacifier in his mouth the whole time. I stood beside his bed and he held my finger with his tiny little hand for hours at a time. He looked at me with pain in his eyes and I felt he looked at mine for comfort. I quickly learned to reset the monitors. They would sound an alarm every time his breathing or heart rate became too slow. I learned when the alarm went off to reset it and stimulate Anthony myself. I could not hold my baby for three days. We had to turn Anthony over from side to side several times a day because the eye closest to the pillow would swell shut. Both of his eyes were black and most of his face had bruises. When the doctor came in and gave him a morphine shot Anthony would look into my eyes with a questioning look as if to ask what is happening to me? Finally on the third day the nurse put a pillow on my lap and laid Anthony there for 20 minutes. I had been breast-feeding him so I had to use a pump and feed him a bottle. Going through this ordeal was very hard for me; I felt so helpless and knew there was nothing I could do to ease his pain or his discomfort. Anthony never cried during this ordeal. He would become restless and whine when his pain medication began to wear off.

That few days we spent in that ICU unit changed my life forever. True faith in God comes from the realization that I can do nothing on my own. I spent several hours listening to babies and children crying and screaming not wanting to be poked or prodded any more. Possibly the crying was tears of fear or the desire for personal touch and for someone to hold them, but no one could. I heard the cries and screams of mothers as their babies died. I saw mothers walking the halls with tears rolling down their faces, possibly praying or just stealing a few moments away to ease their pain. I witnessed all of the frantic commotion as yet another child arrived on the floor at death's door. I thought to myself what would I do without my faith? How would I handle all of this if I didn't have God to turn to in moments like this?

4

THE FIRST YEARS

Anthony recovered from his surgery just fine. When he went for his six-week check-up after the surgery, the surgeon was very pleased with the results. She explained, "He should recover completely and should have no problems developing into a normal healthy little boy". Every where we went the first few weeks after his surgery people said, "Oh My God, what happened to your baby?" They often had a look of horror on their face. Others just gave us the looks but didn't ask. You could clearly see the incision across the whole top of his head. I finally began to put hats on him whenever we went out into public. I was not in any way ashamed of the way he looked. I just got tired of reliving it all every time I had to tell a well meaning stranger his story.

As time went on, our lives seemed to gain a degree of normalcy. When Anthony was just a few weeks old we discovered our son did not like to travel. My family lived about six hours away from us. We decided to take a trip to see my family for a few days. Anthony did not adjust to his new surroundings very well. He would only sleep for 20 minutes at a time every few hours. He cried a lot and was very irritable most of the time we were gone. By the time we returned home I was exhausted. When we arrived home, I took him in and laid him in his crib. He looked around, noticed his surroundings and lights up. He began to smile and kick his feet and coo. I looked down at him, laughed, and said to him, "Oh you're happy to be home". Anthony did not like to go places in the car, even on short trips. It was very difficult to keep him in his car seat for very long. He would scream and tantrum when he wanted out. Most babies love a car ride and it puts most to sleep, not Anthony. These were the first of many signs of irregular behavior.

Most babies love to be cuddled and rocked. Anthony preferred to lie on my lap, but didn't enjoy cuddling or rocking. He would always try to suck on the material of my nightgown, but would not take a pacifier. He often preferred just to be laid down and left alone. Most babies enjoy being in a swing; it will often make them fall asleep. Anthony screamed any time the swing was moving and would become quiet or fall asleep when the swinging stopped.

As time progressed, Anthony met most of the normal childhood Development's right on time. My other children, and most children I know, learned to maneuver a walker by four to six months of age and would be running all over the house in it. Anthony did not like the walker, he only learned to push it backwards a couple of inches he never learned to move it forward. He preferred to be laid on a colorful quilt and left alone. He crawled on time and walked on time and in some ways acted completely normal but deep in my heart I knew there was something different about him.

By the time Anthony reached one year of age I really began to notice there were marked differences between him and other children. I did not know why or what was causing it. We began having more and more problems. Anthony began to tantrum more and more. When I bought new bottles because the other ones were old and worn, he would not accept the new ones. He screamed and refused the new bottle until finally at midnight I went out and dug the old bottles out of the trashcan. I quickly learned if I had to replace anything Anthony used; it could only be replaced with the same exact kind or color. No changes were allowed. I use to always buy a specific brand of pudding cups. If for some reason I bought a different kind he would look the container over and could tell if it was different. He would throw it across the room and scream and tantrum. If for some reason the company changed the label to include New & Improved, or changed the label in any way, he would not accept it, regardless if it were the same product. I sometimes had to keep the old bottle and empty the contents into the old one and throw the new bottle away.

Between the age of one to two years Anthony demonstrated a small amount of speech. He would only use a few words at one time. When he learned a new word he would stop using one of the other words he already knew. I began to wonder if in fact this could possibly be a result of something having gone wrong during his surgery. I wondered if there had been some sort of brain injury to the part of the brain that controlled speech.

Anthony's behavior was different from most children. He acted as if he did not know how to sit and play with toys. He had no imaginative play. I began spending more time trying to teach him how to play with his toys, and showing him how to push a button or how to make things work. Once he learned how to play with something he just sat and repeatedly did the same action over, and over again. He did not try to experiment or play with toys on his own. He did not play with toys appropriately. Instead of pushing a car and making car noises he sat and would turn the car over and repeatedly spin the wheels over and over. He seemed to be lost in his own little world. He would often take his cars or other objects and line them up into rows. I later learned this is called self-stimulation. Anthony was also obsessed with spinning himself. Sometimes he would do it so much that he would make himself sick. It would often be impossible to make him stop.

During this time, Anthony also became obsessed with the movie "The Wizard of Oz". This movie had to be on 24/7. When the movie stopped, it had to be rewound and replayed over and over. If he went to sleep and the movie stopped, he would wake up and scream and tantrum until the movie was put back on. This went on for over two months.

5

THE TERRIBLE TWO'S

The endless days of being over stressed really began to take a toll on me. I was beginning to feel I was going to lose my mind. I was watching television one night and happened to change the channel to a movie. This movie was about a boy with Autism. Although Anthony was not as severe as this child and did not display all of this child's behavior I noticed some remarkable similarities between this child's behavior and mine. This is when I first considered Autism as a possibility.

By the age of two years, Anthony could operate the VCR by himself. He would watch a portion of a movie and then rewind it back and watch the same sequence of the events over and over. Anthony decides he will no longer drink anything but Apple juice, no milk, and no water.

Anthony began going to a childcare home, because I decided to try going back to work. After only a few weeks, we began getting complaints from the owner that our two-year-old child was too aggressive. He would hurt other children totally unprovoked. The owner was concerned for the safety of the other children she cared for. Anthony also demonstrated a lot of aggressive behaviors toward me. He would often hit me, attack me, or pull my hair. If I took him to McDonald's, he would want to play in the play area, but he would not play. He would chase the other children, grab their clothing or lock his arms around their waist and not let go. He would growl, and scare the other children. If I took him shopping, he would growl at children he saw in the store. Shopping with him in stores such as Wal-Mart would often be unbearable. (Someone later told me that this was because the lights in Wal-Mart were too bright, and caused children with Autism to become aggressive because it irritated them).

At two years of age I took Anthony to a neurosurgeon at the children's hospital. I had hoped to get some answers about any possible problems caused by the surgery. The doctor examined his head and even took pictures. This doctor stated, "This was the best job she had ever seen". She even asked permission to send a follow-up with pictures to the doctor that had done his surgery. He still had a small hole on the top of his head, which was considered to be a cranial defect. He has had no complications from this surgery or the defect. I questioned the doctor, "Was there a possibility that any of the problems Anthony displayed, such as delay in speech or behavior problems, could be a direct result of the surgery?" It was her opinion that this was clearly another problem, not related to the surgery. She suggested I seek help from a pediatrician to get some answers.

Finally I called to make an appointment to see a pediatrician requesting an evaluation for Autism. The pediatrician first examined my son, and then he sits down to talk to us. I explained the nightmare we had been living through. I am informed that I am letting my two-year-old child run my home. Can I not see that I have a strong willed child? He then reiterated that Anthony could talk, but would not use words because we made it too easy for him. I had to make him use words to ask for what he wanted or needed. We were to no longer accept the grunts and pointing he used to communicate his wants. The doctor told me if Anthony screamed or would tantrum, not to give in to him no matter what he did. I was to let him scream for hours if necessary. I told the doctor that I had recently returned to work and Anthony had been placed in a daycare home. I expressed the concerns of the day care provider. His only solution was that one of us should stay home and care for Anthony. I decided to give up my job. I left that doctor's office feeling even more discouraged and hopeless. I told myself, "You raised two other children and they turned out fine". "What has happened to you?" I couldn't help feeling that I was a terrible mother. My husband completely agreed with everything the doctor said. It was my fault that Anthony's behavior was out of control. I babied him too much. I gave in to him too much. I was doing everything all wrong. I was told I needed to be firmer and not give in to him. I tried to do everything the doctor, and my husband, instructed me to do. This only made our lives more unbearable.

Anthony's routine was to have that movie going 24 hours a day. When I turned the movie off for him to go to bed he would scream for hours usually until he would make himself sick and fell asleep exhausted. Upon waking only a few short hours later the battle would start all over again. He screamed and cried. I cried right along with him. Whenever he went to the kitchen wanting something, he would grunt and point. I tried to coax him into using words like juice, cheese, or Cheerios. He would only scream and tantrum. Every day became more exhausting, and more of a guessing game. I would spend my day trying to find something to appease him if only for a few moments. I tried everything to follow the doctor's suggestions, but nothing worked. I finally gave up. I would give in just to have some peace. All I wanted was to quiet Anthony and love him just as he was. I couldn't help feeling like I had failed him as a mother. No matter how hard I was trying I wasn't helping him at all. I prayed, "God, what more can I do to understand and help this child?"

As time goes by, some things changed only to bring on new problems. Breaking Anthony from the bottle was almost an impossible task. First, I tried to just take the bottle away, which was a nightmare. Then I began to try harder to introduce the cup. I eventually put only about 1 oz of juice in the bottle and some in the sippy cup. He would drink the juice from the bottle and when it became empty, he would scream and tantrum. Eventually he learned to drink from the cup. I continued to give him the bottle but it was empty, all of the juice was in the cup. He gradually gave up the empty bottle and just drank from the cup. This took several months. He would often twist his finger in his hair as he was falling asleep. Sometimes he would get his finger so tied up in his hair that I had to cut his hair to get his finger free. Later, when he would became upset he no longer twisted his hair but began to twist mine! I had always kept my hair long but began cutting it shorter because he would tangle his finger in my hair until I actually had to cut my hair to get his fingers loose. Most people would say, "Why do you let him do that?" This was Anthony's way of calming or soothing himself instead of self-stimulation. If I refused to let him touch my hair, which I tried to do several times unsuccessfully, he would attack me, scratch, pinch, or bite me. Spanking him only caused him to be more violent toward me. He even scratched my eyeball one time while attacking me. I had to go to the hospital for treatment and I had to wear an eye patch for several days. It hurt for a long time. Thank God there was no permanent damage.

By the time Anthony was 2 1/2 years old, I could really see differences between him and other children his age. These other children were happy, bubbling over with excitement, speaking in sentences. My child was a loner, lined up his toys in a row, or just sat spinning objects. He was obsessed with movie videos and would watch the same one over and over for days, although it now could be turned off when he went to sleep. His speech was a total of eight partial words. He did not say the actual words; he would not sound out the first portion of the word. He would say things like ommy,(mommy) uice,(juice) ovie,(movie) O, (no). He continued to display a lot of aggressive behavior toward me and other family members. If I tried to take Anthony shopping, I had to take him out of his car seat and put him right into the shopping cart in the parking lot. If I waited until I got into the store and then tried to put him into the cart he would throw the biggest, most embarrassing tantrum. He would scream, kick, and fight me like he was a crazed animal. People would stare at me with looks of disgust, like I was abducting my own son, or thinking; can't you control your own son? There were times that I could not calm him down and I would head for the car with him hitting and kicking me. At the age of 2 1/2 years it felt like Anthony was as strong as a man when he became angry.

During this time my husband and I split up and Anthony's father moved 3,000 miles away. I moved in with my mother because I knew I would have to have someone help me take care of Anthony. He was more than a full time job for one person.

Less than a month later I was hospitalized for several days, severely ill. I do not know how my sister and family even managed Anthony since he had never been away from me for even one night. He was difficult to handle and most of my family would be exhausted after just a few short hours. Others tried watching him one time and had a bad experience and would not try again. With Gods help we somehow got through it. It took me several months to recover. But God still had a plan. While I was in the hospital, a social worker set up a counselor to come to my home to see if she could be of any help to me. This woman was an angel sent from God to rescue me out of my situation. Her name was April. The first time she came to see me was just a few days after being released from the hospital. She later told me she had never seen a person that looked so close to death. April came to see me every week. The whole time during our visits Anthony used me as a jungle gym. He never stopped. He was all over me, sometimes hitting me, or trying to choke me. He would throw objects at me from across the room. Believe me he has a pitching arm. It hurt to be hit with metal cars or other hard or heavy objects. God used April to begin opening doors to get help and intervention for Anthony. She referred my case to Central Valley Regional Center. From there a worker came to my home and assessed Anthony and the wheels began to turn. His case had to be reviewed by a panel of doctors and other social workers. They then made a treatment plan. He was qualified to receive help and benefits from their program. They made doctor appointments to get a diagnosis. We finally had an appointment to see a doctor that specialized in diagnosing Autism.

It was getting close to Christmas and my sister decided it would be a good time for us to get away. My sister took Anthony and me to Disneyland, paying for the whole trip. Aren't sisters great? This was Anthony's first trip of this sort so we were not really sure how he would react. We stayed in a hotel the night before. We kept telling him all about Disneyland, Mickey Mouse, and Winnie the Pooh. Anthony had a really hard time falling asleep. At home we did not have a headboard; the bed was just against the wall. This bed at the hotel had a headboard, which really bothered Anthony. He kept trying to push the headboard away. I finally moved him down lower in the bed. We finally settled in for our nightly routine. He began twirling my hair and repeating the word ommy (*meaning mommy*) over and over several times. I would answer, yes Anthony, and he just kept repeating it about 50 times. My sister was about to pull her hair out. She said, "Anthony, everything is OK, it's time to go to sleep now". He just ignored her and kept repeating ommy over and over as if she had never spoken. She was really getting frustrated since he had now been doing this for close to a half hour. She asked me "does he do this every night?" I said, "Yes". She then said, "How do you do this every night?" My answer was very simple, "I don't know how I do it. I just do it".

We tried to prepare Anthony for what was to come, but we didn't really know how he would handle the crowds or the noise. He did really well, and his favorite rides were Dumbo and Alice in Wonderland. A lot of the indoor rides were too loud and he would complain and cover his ears. At one point we were waiting to get on the Casey Jr. Circus

Train, my sister and I were talking and suddenly we heard a man screaming, little boy come here, come here. I turned and looked to see what all of the yelling was about. My look was quickly turned to shock when I realized that Anthony had some how squeezed his little body through the bars of the fence and was now standing on the train track, just steps away from the pond where the Story Book Land Canal Boats went. He had been standing right next to me just a few seconds before. I would have never thought he could have gotten his body through the small opening between the two bars. I panicked. I began trying to coax him back toward us because I knew the train would be coming at any moment. I tried to figure out how to get to him since the gate was locked and the top of each pole of the fence came to a point. Another conductor came from a small booth and pulled him to safety just as the train was pulling up. He held onto Anthony until the train stopped and he could open the gate for me to get him. Oh! If you could have seen some of the looks I got from other parents. Anthony kind of giggled as he climbed onto the train; he was certainly not upset over the whole ordeal, which was more than I could say for his mother at this point. When we got off the train my legs were still limp noodles. I learned a valuable lesson that day. I would never again take my eyes off of him for even one second.

He did very well with the crowds and the noise but he did not like to have to wait in line for our turn to go on the rides. He took a short nap but by 4:30 when we sat down to wait for the parade he became upset. My sister went to get us some food. He noticed that she was gone and began to scream. He fought me and it was hard to keep my hold on him. This lasted about 30 minutes. Other parents just stared at me with a look of disgust watching me fight with him; others tried to help by offering him candy or gum. Their attempts didn't help at all. Finally, when my sister returned and gave him a piece of hot dog for one hand a French fry for the other he stopped screaming and settled down. He has always been close to my sister.

Anthony loved the parade and all the lights, music and dancing. Once the parade was over we headed for the car. Anthony slept part of the way to my nephew's apartment, which was about an hour away. When he woke up he began to scream and there was no calming him down. I finally had to take him out of the car seat. He had been screaming for a while, and we were now only a couple of blocks away from my nephew's apartment. I tried to get him to stop screaming but nothing worked until we were able to get him out of the car. He had a little trouble going to sleep at my nephews. It was all new surroundings again. We had never been there before. The next morning we took him to the Santa Barbara Zoo. He enjoyed the zoo. He growled at the lion. He had the most fun just pushing his stroller around the zoo. When we got on the highway to come home we had not been on the road more than 10 minutes when he started a full-blown tantrum. There was nothing we could do to calm him down or appease him. My sister finally pulled over and I had to get in the back seat with him and lay my head over close to him so that he could play with my hair. I had to ride the whole way home in the back seat with my head leaning over so that he could play with my hair to keep him calmed down. This trip and so many new experiences had definitely left him over stimulated. My sister took about two hours of video on this trip. After watching the whole video I noticed that Anthony did not say one word on this film. He pointed and I used the words for him, explaining or telling him about everything he pointed to.

As I look back now I know I could have never made it through those years without my mother, my sister and God giving me just enough strength to make it through one more day.

6

THE DIAGNOSIS

One month before Anthony turned three years of age we finally got a diagnosis. Autism! Anthony was given this diagnosis by displaying the following symptoms:

1. No imaginative or social play.
2. Impaired ability to make friends with peers.
3. Inability to have a conversation with others.
4. Repetitive use of language.
5. Patterns of interest that was abnormal in intensity or focus.
6. Inflexible adherence to specific routines or rituals.
7. Preoccupation with parts of objects.

Autism is a social disorder that affects every child differently. I am thankful that Anthony was actually diagnosed as high functioning, which meant there was hope for improvement. Anthony was one and a half to two years delayed in almost everything, was sensory sensitive, and considered hyperactive. In the beginning, he was hearing sensitive and then later became partially deaf. He could not stand certain textures on his body or to touch. It was sometimes difficult to keep clothes on him; he pulled his clothing off several times a day. He was orally sensitive to the texture of foods and would not eat very many varieties. He would first smell the food, and then touch it with his tongue before it ever entered his mouth. He could not eat a lot of food because of its texture. He only ate a few basic things; including anything with cheese. To this date he has to have ranch dressing and or ketchup with any food he eats. He has never liked or ate snacks like Twinkies, cupcakes, pastries, cake, or cookies. He only likes plain chocolate candy, no taffy or anything chewy or with nuts and he can't tolerate gum in his mouth. Anthony loves chocolate ice cream with lots of chocolate syrup, but will not eat whip cream on top.

The first feelings I experienced once we received the diagnosis were mixed. I had already pretty much diagnosed him myself by then. OK God, now I know what it's called, but what do I do about it? How do I help him to just be able to cope and make it through one day? I began to read every book I could get my hands on. I thanked God that my child was not as severe as some of the ones I had read about. Some of the books were both scary and depressing. Some of the children I read about ended up being sent to hospitals or special homes because it was too difficult for their families to care for them at home. When my older children and other family members were told of Anthony's diagnosis, it was not really a surprise to anyone. My family and older children have always been supportive in every way they could, and have always tried to help with Anthony and believed the best for him.

The following week I attended a singles group meeting. This was just where God wanted me to be at this particular time. Have you ever felt desperate and you went to a church service and it was totally meant for God to minister to you and your problem? God knew exactly where I was and He met me there. I entered that room that night quite overwhelmed and discouraged. I needed something from God. I was a single mother trying to face all of this alone. There is no known cure for Autism and the doctors don't even know what causes it or prevents it. As I sat there and listened to the minister God spoke to my heart. This minister was telling a story that had taken place some years ago. His son had been in the hospital very ill. Although he was only an infant he was struggling just to stay alive. They were given a diagnosis and told what to expect. This man turned to God on behalf of his son. He put his total faith in God and then reminded God, what His Word says. I Peter 2:24 says "Who his own self bare our sins in his own body on the tree, that we dead to sins should live to righteousness by whose stripes we were healed". (KJV) Anything less than a perfectly normal child was unacceptable to him.

Those words stuck in my mind through the difficult and hard years to come. At that moment I also claimed that healing for my son. Did my faith in God instantly bring about healing for my son? No it did not! But it gave me enough hope to begin a journey of a healing in progress.

I called Anthony's father and begged him to come back and help me take care of him. I felt that now that I actually had a doctor's diagnosis, his father would understand what his son needed and would stop blaming me for the way he was. That is not what happened. He did come back to help, but he had no patience with Anthony, and he would often lose his temper with him. He still continued to blame me as if we had no proof there was something actually wrong with him. He stayed a few months. I ended up pregnant again. Anthony's father had already been considering leaving again and going back to the east coast to work. He was able to make more money working back east. A few weeks after I told him I was pregnant he left again, but promised to come back before the baby arrived. Anthony still continued to use me as a jungle gym. I had an ultrasound at my 12-week check up, there was a heartbeat and everything was good. One week later I became extremely emotionally upset over something that happened to someone close to me. A few days later suffered a very difficult miscarriage.

7

A GOD GIVEN PLAN

This journey took us through months turning into years. I want to share this experience with you so that you can see where we started from and where we are now. I want you to see that by my putting my faith in God, He was then able to work many miracles through my son. By the time you finish this story you should be able to jump for joy. Have I ever given up my faith in God knowing that He would bring about my son's complete healing? No I have not! I still hold God to that promise. I still have faith. Has my faith in God instantly made this journey a breeze? Not hardly!

With God's help I started working on a plan trying to figure out what things needed to be worked on first in order to make our life at home more manageable. Anthony and I began to work with a behaviorist. I was taught some very important tools. I was taught the important behavioral technique called re-direction. Re-directing is when you take the child out of an upsetting situation and get him involved in doing something else. This tool is used when he was getting frustrated or upset because he was not getting what he wanted. It could also used for self-stimulating behavior, like spinning himself, the wheels on a car, or lining up his toys in a row.

I have learned a lot about Autism and how it affects Anthony personally. Since every child is different, every case is different to some degree. I began working hours a day with him using cue cards with pictures, numbers, shapes and colors. We cut pictures out of magazines and glued them to cue cards. We talked about what was in the picture, what it did, went to, or what it was used for. By doing this for hours daily Anthony soon began to say more words. I quickly learned that Anthony had to know what to expect or know what was going to happen in any situation. He would watch the same movie over and over until he knew what to expect or what would be said next. Knowing and understanding this about him has helped me to be able to prepare him for change. This included every day plans as well as trips.

We were planning a trip to Las Vegas because my oldest son was getting married. I started talking about the trip two weeks before we were supposed to go. We looked up pictures of Las Vegas on the Internet. I showed him pictures of our hotel, and what our room would look like. We then made a paper chain to count the days. The trip went as planned; we arrived and checked into our room. It was still daylight. Anthony kept shaking his head and saying O (*meaning no*) aus egas, I would say yes Las Vegas. He would just shake his head no again. I did not understand. We went out for a while and ate dinner and had some fun. When we returned to the room, Anthony ran to the window, it was now dark outside. He was so excited jumping up and down saying aus egas, aus egas. I said yes, Las Vegas. I realized that all of the pictures that I had shown him from the Internet were all pictures that had been taken at night.

He still did not travel well, and would want out of his car seat after just a few minutes, and would sometimes experience carsickness. He really does not like to travel after it gets dark, he has to have a light on in the car all the time if we go anywhere after dark. I learned to try to prepare him for everyday trips to the post office, grocery store, places like Walmart, or the bank. He always needed to be prepared for where we were going and what to expect. There is a very important tip that I want to add here. In the special education class that Anthony attended, they used picture boards in every different part of the room and there was a board on the front door where they entered the room. They made these boards by taking a large piece of poster board paper, and then they laminated the poster board and then glued two strips of Velcro from the top to the bottom of the poster board. When the child entered the room, they would place their things, such as a change of clothes and diapers, jacket, or anything they had brought to school that day in the cubby with their picture on it. They did not use their name but their picture instead. Most of the children could not recognize their name but could recognize their own picture. They then had to go and take their picture off the picture board on the door and place it on another board at the end of their cubby's, which meant they were there. Once they took their picture at the front door and went to the place where the board was at the end of the cubbies, this board would have another picture telling them which area to go to next. So they would take the picture of where they were to go next off that board and place their picture on that board. Then they would proceed to the next area, and place this picture on the board in this area. This could be a picture of the round table, the play area, computer lab, the reading area or the red carpet. During the time that they were in that area, a class aid would take those pictures off the board and replace them with a picture of the area they were to go to next. She would put a picture of the next area on that board for each child, so she put 8 pictures of the red carpet on that board. When their time was up in one area they had to get the picture of the next area off the board and go to the next area and put that picture on the poster board and then complete the task for that area. Then, a class aide would come along and take those pictures off and replace them with the picture of the area they were to go to next. This was the same routine everyday. The children had to learn to follow the routine. Everyday they did not always go to every area in the same order, the areas were changed, but the children did not seem to get upset because they had that picture showing them where to go. Children with Autism always want the same routine. As difficult as it may be, you are not benefiting your child if you always give into them. You can make routines at home, but they also need to learn coping skills to be able to handle things when there is a situation that has to be changed. Children with autism are visual learners; they understand things or remember things by pictures in their mind. A very wonderful woman that I met through group meetings with the Autism Society had three sons affected with autism at different levels. She once told me that she went and took pictures of the grocery store, the bank, the Post Office, Walmart, the gas station, McDonald's, their schools, and anywhere else they went to on a regular basis. When she was preparing to leave her home she put the pictures on her picture board on her door showing her children where they were going. She said she sometimes still had some minor upsets but for the most part it eased their mind to have that picture there so they knew what to expect. I didn't really learn too much about this until later after we had worked through that problem. When I put Anthony into the car he would often repeat where we were going over and over several times. He would ask me and then repeat it again and again until we arrived there. I think he would repeat it until he found the picture in his mind. I quickly found out he could handle two or three different stops but more than that was to much and if I tried a fourth place I often had to turn around and go back to the car because he would throw a tantrum and I could not get control.

8

CHOOSING YOUR BATTLES

Many people told me that I would have to give in a lot or fight with my child constantly, so I learned to choose my battles. One battle I always choose is if my child is doing something harmful to himself or others, there is no way that this behavior will be tolerated. It can sometimes be a battle to teach them that such behavior may cause them to hurt themselves, other people, or animals and that this will not be tolerated. We have tried several pets in our home over the years and most we had to get rid of because Anthony would hurt them. I was told very early on that if I could not teach Anthony to respect my space, and teach him not to show violent behavior toward me, that by the time he reached 10 or 12 years of age I may have to place him in a home for the developmentally disabled. I would not be able to handle him at home. There was the possibility that he would really hurt me physically as he got older and stronger. I made two choices a long time ago. One choice was I would never allow the doctors to medicate Anthony in order to make my life easier. I have heard too many horror stories of children that have grown up on medications used to control them or their behavior. There have been many stories about what that medication was like for the child. The second choice I made was no matter what intervention it took; Anthony would never be put in a home. My sister said that would never happen to him as long as she was alive.

At a very young age Anthony recognized the streets we took to get somewhere. He could direct people which way to go if he was riding with them. Anthony would often try to direct which way I went while driving. He would point in the direction he wanted me to go, he would scream and tantrum if I went a different way. Whenever anyone came to see us, he had to always walk them outside and he had to be the one to tell everyone which way to go, he would point showing them the direction he wanted them to go when they left. Most of the time he would not let them go the way they needed to go. If they did not follow his directions, he would scream and tantrum and throw a fit right there in the front yard for sometime. Most of the time everyone just learned to go around the block and come out on the other side and then go the way they needed to go. Anthony didn't make life easy for anyone. He would often try to make people sit where he wanted them to sit. At the dinner table people were only allowed to sit where he wanted you to sit or he would tantrum. Anytime I sat down, he was on me, climbing all over me, getting behind me, pushing me with his feet, or choking me from behind. If I got up and moved to another chair or the couch he was right back on top of me.

We have been through numerous hours of behavior therapy, speech therapy, and occupational therapy to work on his fine motor skills such as writing, buttoning, and cutting, and his sensory sensitivities. At this point Anthony did not have a dominant hand. He would work with one hand and when it got tired he would switch to the other hand. If he were tracing an object he would trace around the right side with the right hand and then switch hands and trace the left side of the object with his left hand. He had therapy for that too. They also tried to help him learn to tolerate things he was sensitive to, such as swinging on a swing, digging for toys in a bin of uncooked rice, and playing with whip cream, which he really did not mind but just begged every two seconds to go wash his hands. I also learned that he was very sensitive to smell. We could never understand why when he was a baby and we would eat breakfast at a restaurant, he would always fuss or cry from the moment we sat down. We would try holding him or giving him a bottle or toys, but nothing worked. Very often, one of us would have to take him outside while the other person ate their food and then we would change places. I ate a lot of cold food over the years. As he got older, he could never eat breakfast at a restaurant. He always complained of feeling sick. He now orders a grilled cheese sandwich or something else but will never eat breakfast food at a restaurant, even if it is early morning.

I also learned a technique called brushing. You take a surgical brush and very gently do strokes over certain parts of the body. Ten strokes on the arms, legs, back, chest and stomach area; and then apply lotion. This desensitizes him. In other words, when he is upset or over stimulated this technique helps to calm his senses down and he is once again able to cope and get control of himself. It worked wonders for him.

We sometimes had an extreme problem out of the blue. One time when I was helping Anthony put toothpaste on his toothbrush; he began to throw a fit. He could not stand that Barney turned upside down when you turned the tube of toothpaste over to use it. I actually had to cover up Barney. This had never happened before and went on for a few days and then it became no problem at all once again. I noticed he could not handle things as well if he was tired, or had already done too many different things that day.

Anthony has gone through a lot of testing. He had an EEG to check for any sort of seizure disorder. Seizure disorders are very common in children diagnosed with autism. Sometimes when Anthony would fall asleep his body would jerk involuntarily. His EEG was normal with no signs of any type of seizure disorder. He also went through metabolic testing to see if there was another problem causing the autistic symptoms. His metabolic testing came back normal. This proved there was not a metabolic problem causing his autistic symptoms. He actually was autistic. Extensive hearing tests revealed that he was partially deaf in both ears. He had ear surgery and had tubes put in to correct the problem. The ear doctor informed us after the surgery that there was a thick glue type substance in his ear canals. After the tubes were put in his hearing increased a great deal. He then began to see a speech specialist. This continued for several months and improved his speech greatly. He also had to be sedated and had his front teeth capped because the apple juice had eaten all the enamel off of his front teeth. They then did all the other dental work he needed as well. At the age of three and a half years Anthony was partially toilet trained.

My family was always loving, supportive, understanding and patient in dealing with Anthony's difficulties. My family had to learn to accommodate him during family functions and group settings. For a family holiday gathering Anthony took his own movies and toys in his backpack. My sister kept a supply of children's movies and toys and coloring supplies for all the children to use that visited her home.

Anthony would usually go right from the front door straight back to a bedroom where he was allowed to watch movies and play with his toys. Almost all of our family gatherings took place at my sister's house. Usually Anthony would be playing or watching a movie and family members one at a time would go in and spend time with him. He loved to be with the family, but was not able to deal with everyone at once. He would sometimes sneak out of the bedroom and would crawl under the dining room table, or hide behind furniture, and watch what was going on. As he got older he began to adjust and gradually began coming out and associating with the group more, especially if there were other children there. He would sometimes come out for a little while, and then retreat back to the bedroom again.

Anthony attended a special education class for several months. He was a lot higher functioning then most of the children in his class. His teacher completed an evaluation and called a new IEP meeting. His teacher and the head of Special Education decided he would benefit more from a normal preschool classroom. The first time that we tried this, it was a difficult battle. He would often scream and tantrum and tried to hurt some of the staff. I would leave him crying, kicking, and screaming and I would cry all the way home. A lot of the time the staff would have to call me because he had been screaming or throwing a tantrum for over an hour and I would have to go back to school and pick him up. Anthony never demonstrated this behavior in the special education class. He never cried or was upset and he did not tantrum at all, even on his first day. It was difficult for him to adjust to the different class and most of the children only spoke Spanish, so most of the time the staff would talk to them only in Spanish. I finally decided that this was not of any benefit for Anthony. I was concerned that his severe reaction to the different arrangement would cause him to go into regression. I felt the confusion caused by two different languages would only cause more confusion with his speech. We were trying so hard to work on his speech and improve the sounds of his words. I felt that being exposed to so much Spanish was only making our problems worse. I really didn't know much about Anthony's rights or mine during this time. Even though I didn't agree with this placement, I didn't know how to get them to change it. I thought that they knew what was best and I was just supposed to go along with what they decided. I understood that space in the special education classes is limited, but I still didn't feel that this placement was an appropriate learning environment for

Anthony at this time. It was very frustrating and I pulled him out of that class and we took a break from school for a while.

After a few months, I decided once again to try another normal preschool class. This brought on a whole new problem. When Anthony was supposed to arrive at school all of the preschool children from five different classes were on the playground playing. He would get to the gate and could not go on to the playground. All the other children were running, playing and screaming. The noise level was very loud. I even tried to stay with him until all the children went into their classes. He could not tolerate this at all. We ended up having to change their routine to accommodate him. I began taking him to school later after the children had all gone into their own classrooms. He could now walk onto the playground and everything was quiet, he could then go into his classroom, be with the other children, and was able to cope much better. He did very well in this classroom setting. The only real problem we had was that there were some children that beat up on him, kicking him in the legs and the groin area. He was tested while he was at this school and his teachers told me that academically he was at a first grade level. He eventually adjusted and was able to go and play with the other children on the playground in the morning before his class started. This took some time and effort on my part. I began to take him a couple of minutes earlier every few days. This process took several months. This class was still bilingual; although they did give some instruction in Spanish on an individual basis they used English when addressing the whole class.

When you have a child with this disorder the main tool you need to survive is "patience". There are no easy fixes. There is no getting over it quickly. It all takes time, and more time, and more time.

Anthony and I were still living with my mother. We went to stay at my older son's house to help out for a few weeks. My son was recovering from a vehicle accident and my daughter in law was pregnant and having a hard time. Anthony was running and fell and hit the bumper of my son's car knocking out his front teeth. Anthony went back to the dentist and he was able to recap the small portion of teeth Anthony still had left. This ordeal was very upsetting to Anthony. He called his father and kept telling him I need you to come here. His father quit his job and moved back to be closer to Anthony.

Anthony was sick all the time. He had chronic ear infections, and seemed to catch every virus he was exposed to. As he got older his sleeping pattern became more difficult to handle. He would fall asleep and sleep for a couple of hours, awake for several hours, go back to sleep for a couple of hours and then wake up, and want to stay up. Anthony's behaviorist advised me, that when he woke up that I should not get out of bed or let him get out of bed. I was to give him no stimulation like turning on the light or TV. I hardly got any sleep during these times. He never slept all night. Sometimes when he woke up he would say ommy or other words over and over for hours. Sometimes he would play with my hair and accidentally pull it. I would keep telling him, go back to sleep. Sometimes I would dose off and he would move and wake me up. Sometimes he would lie there without making a sound for several hours. I would think he had fallen asleep but I would look at him and his eyes would be wide open. Occasionally, he would wake up and go right back to sleep. These nights were few and far between. I was exhausted all the time. Sometimes my mom would try to watch him so I could take a nap, but he would repeatedly wake me up. He would never take naps either, even when he was young.

9

PROGRESS ONE STEP AT A TIME

When Anthony was four years old we went through a period of time where he went from one virus to another until he had been sick for six weeks straight. It seemed like as soon as he would begin to feel better, all of a sudden his fever would shoot up again. Then he got a virus that caused sores in his mouth and on his tongue. He could not stand to eat or drink. We were in the doctor's office every few days. We tried to give him a medication to help clear up the infection in his mouth. This medication must have burned or something because he became like a crazed animal. He would growl and scratch anyone who came near him. He ran to the bathroom and turned on us. He tried to scratch at me. He would not let me get near him. He tried to push the door shut but I got my foot in the way and the door was open a little. He leaned up against the door and kept trying to push the door closed. I put something in the way to keep the door open a little bit. I sat down on the other side of the door and started talking to him very softly to get him to calm down. I told him I threw the medicine away and I would not give it to him anymore. I kept trying to get him to come out. I put my hand inside the door a little so I could try to touch him but he would growl at me. After some time, I was gradually able to inch the door open and move more of my body into the bathroom with him. I prayed and prayed for God's guidance on what to do. I just kept inching my way into the bathroom and then I sat a few feet away still continuing to tell him everything was going to be okay. I was finally able to reach out to him. He crawled into my lap like a ball. He nestled there and refused to leave my side. I had to hold him on my lap, even when I used the bathroom. He would stand at the side of the bathtub crying while I quickly showered. He would not leave me for one second. He would not let his father or my mom even touch him or do anything for him. I often wondered if I would make it through this ordeal. He got so bad that he regressed to a vegetable state. He just lay on the couch or sat on my lap and constantly made a groaning sound like humming or whining. He did this every minute he was awake. He would only sleep for ten to twenty minutes every few hours. If he woke up and I was not right there, he would start screaming and would continue on for hours, although I was there holding him. I constantly tried to get food or anything down him but he would take nothing. He stopped asking to go the bathroom. He stopped using words at all. He had always loved to take a bath. When he felt sick, he would often ask to take one several times a day. He would not take a bath. He would not let me hold him and give him a bath. If I tried to bathe him, he would act like a crazed animal again. So every once in a while I would get a washcloth with warm water and try to wash him little by little. He would only allow this for couple of minutes, then his whine would become louder and louder, and I would have to stop. If family members or anyone came over he would just sit on my lap and cover his head with a blanket and continue on with his moan. I finally took him to the hospital even though he had been seeing his pediatrician every few days. I had reached the end of my rope. I felt if someone did not do something to intervene; my child might never come out of this vegetable state. They gave him a shot for pain and a strong antibiotic shot. They found out that the cause of this severe regression was that he was severely dehydrated. If I had not taken him to the hospital when I did, he could have died. I was upset that his pediatrician had not done this sooner. Spending those few hours in that emergency room that night hooked up to the IV seemed to rejuvenate him and he began to act more like himself again. It started him on the road to recovery. He had lost so much weight that his skin just hung on his bones and you could see all of his rib cage. It took some months for him to fully recover and gain the weight back. It took some time for his speech to come back, and it took several months to get him partially toilet trained again.

Anthony's dad left and moved back to the east coast again. He tried to tell me that I just didn't know what it was like for him. He said, "When a man finds out that he is having a son, you have all these expectations of what your son will grow up to be and do, and how he will follow in your footsteps. It is difficult to accept that your son will never be "Normal" like other kids". He said, "I am not sure that I can accept him the way he is. I know he will never fulfill the dreams I had for him." I just shook my head and asked him how he could even say that. I said, "I love Anthony the way he is, he does not have to be a certain way or do anything in particular to get me to love or accept him. I love him unconditionally. I'm sorry but I don't understand how you can feel that way." Up until this point I kept trying to get him to love and accept Anthony. I wanted him to try to understand him and take a look at who he really was on the inside. I wanted him to be more of a father to him. I realized that day that he may never be in his life more then just on a visitation basis.

In the summer, I moved out of my mom's house and rented a house for Anthony, my daughter, and my self. I started trying to work with Anthony to get him to sleep in his own room. No matter how hard I tried, he was not going to do this at this time. He had been sleeping in bed with me for almost three years. He just could not adapt to this.

Anthony became completely toilet trained. I still kept him in Pull Ups at night for a while. We then tried to stop doing that altogether. He would not give them up. He insisted on wearing the Pull Up at night even though he never wet one. During this time, I made crafts and sold them in a craft booth. I also got a license for a day care home. I felt I needed to be on my own taking care of my family the best I could. Anthony did not adapt well to other children coming into our home and taking my time and attention. I tried watching children of different ages. He could not get along with any of them. It became more of a battle everyday. It was causing him to fight with the other children and he became non-compliant with me. I finally gave up and closed the day care.

When the following school year started, Anthony went to his second special education class, which was considered to be pre-kindergarten. The children ranged in ages from four to seven years old. He did quite well in this class. He actually tried to help the teacher and the other children. Most of the violent behavior subsided. He was very gentle and helpful to the other disabled students in his class. He learned a lot of new words, word structure, and two or three word phrases. He excelled in academics. He rode a handicap bus that picked him up at home and brought him home when his class was over. The only real problem we had was that they changed bus drivers almost everyday. Two or three times a week they would try to drop him off at another house down the street with the same address. He would try to give them directions and tell the driver they had the wrong house. The driver would not pay any attention to him. They would sometimes sit in front of the wrong house honking for several minutes. A lot of times they would radio in to dispatch that there was no one home. The transportation dispatch would call me and I would go outside and could see the bus down the street. I would tell them to radio them back, and tell them that they were in front of the wrong house. I would stand in front of my house frantically waving at the bus driver. By the time Anthony actually arrived home he was hysterical. I would call transportation back and urged them to give better instructions because I did not want my child going through this everyday. The transportation people got to know my voice very well and could recognize me when I called. First, I talked to dispatch. Then I started complaining to supervisors. I finally went to the person that controlled the whole Transportation Department. This man began trying to fix the problem, but it had taken me several weeks. He than began calling me everyday to check to see that everything was okay. Occasionally, we had a problem. He improved the bus driver's instructions and was finally able to stop the problem completely.

10

A GIANT LEAP FOR ONE LITTLE BOY

Anthony had made so many improvements, in so many ways over the past few months. As the months continued to pass he constantly showed more improvements in several areas. When Anthony turned five years old, he was retested and was cleared to go into a regular kindergarten class starting in the fall. He could now say the alphabet and recognize each letter and could tell you what they were. He could spell his first and last name when asked. He could count up to 25 and could identify numbers up to 10 even if they were not in order. He could write his first name, although it was sloppy. He could identify all the shapes and colors. He was approved for a regular kindergarten class without an aide or assistance. He had tested at first grade level in most areas of the curriculum they used.

He had a very large vocabulary and now spoke where most people could understand about 98% of what he was saying. He was one big smile, full of energy, and talked constantly. He was happy, well adjusted, and would now go up to other children and introduce himself and ask them if they wanted to play with him or be his friend. To a person that knew nothing of his history, he seemed like any other normal boy. I look at him and smile and thank God everyday for all the improvement he has made. God is wonderful and having faith in Him causes miracles to happen.

Anthony went back to the dentist; once again they put him to sleep and did all of his dental work. He than began to have hearing problems again and his tonsils were always swollen to the point of almost closing the back of his throat. I took him out of the special education class and he had surgery again. This time they inserted ear tubes and removed his tonsils and adenoids. His father came for the surgery, and stayed a few days to help care for him. I had read information that was published about children with Autism who had had their adenoids removed; it claimed their autistic symptoms improved a great deal. I had no idea of Anthony's expectation of the surgery. It's sort of funny. Anthony was really disappointed after having this surgery that he still was not able to speak Spanish. He said, "I thought when I had this surgery that after I came out I would be able to speak Spanish and I can't". Having this surgery improved Anthony's health a great deal. He wasn't sick constantly anymore. He no longer had ear and throat infections. His speech improved, he ate better, slept better, and had more energy. It was almost like night and day. His behavior improved almost overnight.

It had always been difficult to keep any weight on him and I had a lot of trouble just trying to keep him at 40 lbs. Every time he got sick he would easily drop 5 lbs that he could not afford to lose. It would take me a couple of months to get the weight back on him that he had lost. I decided to try something different. I put him on a SLIM-FAST diet plan. I gave him one shake every morning. I think drinking this shake gave him the vitamins he was lacking in the food he ate. He began to eat more foods and seemed to be hungry all the time. Up to this point he would ask for food and eat a few bites and didn't want any more. At lunch and dinner, I gave him a plate with a few choices. He would usually choose one thing on the plate and eat that entire portion, and then he would say he was done. He began to eat more of the food on his plate and gradually had worked up to requesting seconds or thirds. He is now able to maintain a healthy weight and his rib cage didn't stick out anymore.

After Anthony recovered from his surgery, I gave up my house, put my stuff in storage, and took him back east to see his dad for a month, during the summer before he was to go back to school. I knew once he started school he would not be able to see his dad much. Anthony flew on an airplane for the first time. He did very well. By the last half hour he began to get agitated and wanted off the plane. I felt this was minor since the flight took six hours. We actually ended up staying for two months because I became ill. I was advised by the doctor to stay in bed and rest for the next two weeks and not to drive home for six weeks. Anthony really enjoyed visiting with his father. We enjoyed days at the beach and other outings.

I bought a new car and Anthony and I began our journey home four weeks later. We traveled all the way across the United States. I was not sure how Anthony would handle the trip. He had gotten better at traveling but we had never been on a driving trip of this magnitude before. I put Anthony in the middle of the back seat so that he could see where we were going, hopefully minimizing carsickness. He had a box full of his favorite toys and books right next to him and his favorite blanket. We stopped at almost every rest area and played catch or we would throw a Frisbee around to get him to release some of his energy so he could cope with being in the car and in his car seat without becoming agitated. We talked, sang songs, and told stories to pass the time. I also pointed out interesting things we saw along the way or I sometimes told him to look for things to occupy his mind and keep him busy. We stayed at Days Inn the first night, and from then on, whenever he saw a Days Inn sign he would ask, "Are we stopping here?" Sometimes we had only been on the road an hour. Every time he saw a Days Inn sign, he wanted to stop now. I continually promised him we would stop before it gets dark. When it was getting close to the time for us to stop, I always told him, "Anthony, find us a Days Inn to stop at". He would search the signs and when he found one, we stopped. He did great as long as it was a Days Inn every night. He still likes things to be done in routine or the same patterns. He did a lot better than I expected. We drove all day and would sometimes be in the car for several hours at a time. He was a real trooper. The last day he started to complain and I just kept reminding him we would be home tonight. He never experienced any significant carsickness. It was a journey to remember, that he and I will never forget.

Anthony had made so much progress over the past year I honestly felt he would be able to face life's challenges and come out a winner. He made so much progress physically, emotionally, and mentally. He also began to accelerate academically, which made me believe that with God's help one day he would be fully recovered from Autism.

11

GOD IS STILL WORKING HIS PLAN

When we returned home I moved back in with my mother. Anthony started kindergarten. He was put into a class that had both English and Spanish speaking children. He had problems with the teacher talking in Spanish to the other children who did not speak English because he could not understand her. This really bothered him. He would come home and complain that she was talking to him but he could not understand what she was saying. I went with him to talk to the teacher and she explained to him that if she was using words that he could not understand, she was not talking to him. This seemed to relieve his mind.

Anthony's father and I continued to converse by phone after we returned home from visiting him over the summer. A few months later, we decided to get remarried. Anthony, my 18 year old daughter and I would move back to the east coast with him. I sold most of our belongings, and packed what little we had left into a small truck. My older son drove the truck to Las Vegas for me. Anthony's father met us there, we got married, and he drove the truck with our belongings back to his home on the east coast. This was the worst mistake I ever made in my whole life. I kept feeling that I shouldn't go through with the wedding and I wanted to back out, but I didn't. We had barely said I do when things began to go wrong. He started treating my daughter and me bad the very first day. The next five days on the road was hell for all of us. I wanted to turn around and go home, I cried for most of the trip. I felt I had been deceived and lied to about everything. The situation continued to get worse with each passing day. We got to the east coast and tried to settle in. My daughter and Anthony both had their own rooms. I got Anthony registered in school. He seemed to adapt well even with so many changes. Anthony slept in his own room in his bed every night except once when he was sick. He said he did this to show his father how grown up he was and because he didn't want to disappoint him. He never complained or cried about it. I would lay down with him until he went to sleep. When he woke up in the middle of the night, which was often, I would go back to his bed and lay with him until he fell back to sleep.

It had only been a few weeks and our marriage relationship continued to get worse. One day my husband called me from work to tell me that his employer was sending him out of the state to work for the next two to three months. He packed and left. He was just gone a couple of days when I was served an eviction notice, and shut off notices from the power company, and the cable got turned off since he hadn't paid any of the bills. I checked the checking account to arrange to pay the bills and discovered it was over drawn by hundreds of dollars. I called my husband in tears. My husband suggested I get money from my family in order to keep a roof over our heads and to get the heat and power bills paid and everything in order by the time he got home. I called my family and cried telling them what a mistake I had made. My family rallied together and made a plan to get us back home.

I secretly packed our things, keeping everything hidden from Anthony so he wouldn't tell his dad we were leaving on the phone if he talked to him. His father had made too many threats in the past; I wasn't taking any chances on getting my kids out of there safely. One day Anthony came home from school and I had pulled out all the boxes I had packed and hidden from him. We were ready to load. My older son flew in to help with driving the truck. We picked him up at the airport and I had the movers waiting to load the truck when we got home. We got the truck loaded and left there in the middle of the night. We were finally on our way home. We left there without my being able to prepare Anthony for this trip at all. I knew that this was going to make it very hard for him to cope. Anthony did not know everything that was going on, it was difficult for me to try to explain to him why we were doing what we were doing; sometimes there are things you just can't tell a five-year-old child. The first day he was extremely upset and carsick, he couldn't understand why I was taking him away from his dad. The rest of the trip continued to be difficult for him too. I wish there had been a way to handle things differently, but Anthony's father had made too many threats and I was in his house, it was too dangerous to do it any other way. I left the east coast having been married a little over a month but did not file for divorce again until some time later.

We arrived back home and we moved in with my mom again. I took Anthony back to get him in the same school he was in before. He wanted to go back into the same class he was in before we left, but this class was now full. They told us he would have to go into another class where he didn't know the teacher or any of the students. Everyday became a battle. He cried, screamed, and begged for me to take him home. He complained that he felt sick. I would try to take him to the different class and he would grab a hold of the nearest pole and wrap his arms and legs around it and hold on as tight as he could. I had to be physically forceful to get him to let go of the pole. There was not one day that I was actually able to get him into that new class. After several days of this, I went and talked to the Principal about the situation. I begged them to let him go back to the other class because Anthony or I could not stand to go through this routine everyday. The Principal talked to the teacher, and although her class already exceeded State limits, they agreed to let him back into her class. He was too upset to stay that day so we went home. The next day we went back and he went right into the old class. He was happy and smiling and had no problems. I kissed him good-bye and he went into his class happy.

Anthony never kissed anyone. He would sometimes let grandma or I kiss his cheek but he wouldn't kiss back. From the time he was little he would never let me kiss his boo boo's. I could ask if he wanted me to blow on it and sometimes he did, but would never let anyone kiss the place he hurt. I would ask, "Can I kiss it?" He would give me a strange look, and say no, that's not going to help anything.

An office job came open at the company where my older son worked. I took them my resume. I was called back for two interviews, and got the job. This would the first job I had outside the home since Anthony was two years old. I took the job. On my lunch hour, I would drive though neighborhoods trying to decide where I wanted to live. I picked the school that I felt God lead me to for Anthony. I then searched for open apartments in that area. I found an area I really liked. I drove around several times before I was able to run into someone who could tell me who rented these apartments. I went to the rental office but was told they had nothing available. I felt this was where God had led me. I was so disappointed. I just kept praying about it. The following Sunday at church, I requested prayer that God would open the door for us to get a place that would be safe for us to live. A man in my prayer circle prayed the most awesome prayer for me. A few days later, I felt I should call the rental office again. When I did, the receptionist told me that they had an unexpected move out. She explained that she had already received an application from some other people that were interested in the apartment, and that the other applicant had first choice for the apartment if they were approved. I went into the rental office, filled out an application, and kept praying. I waited two days and called back. The other people had backed out. She asked me to bring in some verification of my income. I took it and dropped it off on my way to work the next day. About thirty minutes later, they called to say I had been approved and could come in, put down my deposit, and move in the following week.

We moved in. My new apartment was about twenty miles from my mother. My older son lived in the same town but a few miles away on the other side of town. I felt so blessed. I felt God had moved things around to allow me to live where I wanted. I didn't have much to move since I had sold most of my belongings, before going back east. God blessed us and he soon provided everything we needed. I slowly ended up with a house full of new furniture. God is awesome.

We sometimes face stumbling blocks in life, when we least expect it. The following Monday morning I took Anthony to the new school to register him. We were both excited, but there was a problem. All of the kindergarten classes were full. There was no room for him. I even talked to the Principal hoping that would help. We were told we had no choice; he would have to go to another school a few blocks away. They offered to put him on a waiting list and as soon as there was an opening at that school they would call me. Anthony was quite upset. I had prepared him to start that school, not another school. We went to the other school. He was upset, but decided to stay and I promised to meet him at the door when his day was finished, then take him to daycare. He did pretty well and got through the first day. As the next few weeks passed, everyday he came home complaining, this teacher was mean to him and yelled at him. I tried talking to her and her attitude toward me was not much better. Everyday, she had nothing but negative things to say. She kept telling me he was too far behind and would never catch up with her class. She said that he was delayed more than any other student in her class. This woman made me feel like I had failed my child as a parent. I turned to God and prayed for his help. I felt that God had wanted him at the other school. A few weeks later, the first school called to say they had an opening for him. I really prayed. I knew that he had gone through so many changes in such a short time. I wasn't sure he could handle another one so soon. I prayed some more and felt God wanted me to change him back to the first school. I talked to him and he was very excited to go back to the other school. He adjusted well and went right into the new class and school. We had moved three times and he had gone to four schools in just a few short months. I had also began working full time, he was now separated from me even more hours a day. But God had a plan. The new teacher was great. She never raised her voice at him. She had only positive things to say about him. She began to tutor him two afternoons a week on her own time to help him catch up, and he did. He excelled and was able to maintain his school level. He even was able to sing on stage with his classmates when his class performed for the kindergarten program. The next few months were full of major adjustments for both of us. Working full time outside the home was hard for both of us to get used to. Up until this point, just caring for Anthony was my full time job without working a full time job too. He missed me terribly and I missed him, but Anthony did great through the rest of the year. He graduated and was approved to go into first grade.

Anthony played baseball for the first time. He was great and loved playing against the other teams. He made a lot of friends. This was the first time we had tried a sport. We would often meet other children from his team in a store and he would go up and talk to them. He was making a network of friends.

He also made friends with the kids that went to the children's room during my singles meetings. The teacher in that class is a grandmother type. She adores Anthony. She always hugged him and kissed his head. When he completed baseball, he had to take his trophy to show her. She ranted and raved about how proud she was of him. If we missed some meetings, she would always be so happy to see him and would tell him she missed him so much. Everyone from my singles group adopted him. He was the one child everyone loved. We often went out as a group to get something to eat. Anthony begged to go. He always had to sit with the men. There was this one man who had cerebral palsy. He was Anthony's best friend. They would often sit together. He was fun and silly and Anthony loved to play along with him. He taught Anthony how to throw small balls of paper at people and then turn the other way like you didn't do it. Our group often got together at this mans house. A lot of times children were not allowed to come, but this man told me Anthony was always welcome in his home. God has been faithful in providing Anthony with great men in his life since he only sees his dad a couple of weeks a year.

Through the summer, I did not want Anthony to become lazy or get out of the pattern of a structured environment. He had made so much progress and I wanted him to continue to do that. I put him in Montessori School for the summer. He enjoyed making new friends and continued to learn. Their classes are very structured but Anthony got to make choices about what project he wanted to do. He adjusted well but sometimes he really missed me a lot. Even though the cost was more than I could afford I felt it was worth it. They studied Dinosaurs, which are Anthony's favorite thing. Sometimes I give him money to put in a wishing well. I ask him what did you wish for and he always says that God would bring dinosaurs back to life so he could see them.

The people I worked with were great. They were very understanding about Anthony. If he was sick, had a problem at school, or had a day out of school, they would let me bring him to work with me. They all talked to him like he was part of the family. I tried not to do that too much. He loved to go to work with me though. It felt great that my employer allowed me to still be the mom he needed me to be and hold down a full time job. God has blessed me there.

12

THE REST OF THE STORY

Anthony went for his first grade physical. He seemed to be doing great. He could not pass the eye exam. They told me that one of his eyes had a tendency to drift. I took him to an eye doctor. He said that everything looked good but Anthony's eye muscles were under developed. He said that this was probably a direct result from the Autism. He would need to wear glasses to read or to do sight work. He also showed me exercises that I could do with Anthony at home to help improve his eye muscles.

Anthony started first grade. Once again God worked His plan. He loved his teacher and made many new friends in his class. After the first month or so I requested to talk to the teacher. I noticed while he was doing his homework, he transposed numbers and letters a lot. I voiced my concerns to his teacher. I asked if she felt it was necessary to test Anthony for Dyslexia. She wasn't concerned, and explained to me that testing was not necessary. Many children start out at the beginning of the year transposing numbers and letters but most have quit doing it on their own by the end of first grade. If he continued to do that by the end of the school year she promised to have him checked. By the end of first grade he no longer had that problem.

She gave me some wonderful news. She told me that he had been selected from her class of 20 students to participate in a special reading program. She told me that he had been selected for no particular reason. I knew that God had His hand in this. Anthony was tutored one on one for a half hour everyday. When he began working with the tutor he was at reading level 2. She worked with him for several months. Our goal for him was to reach level 5 but he reached level 7 and was dropped from the program. We would be riding in the car and he would read signs that we passed on the side of the road. He reads really well now and he loves for me to read bible stories about Jesus to him at night.

In October, Anthony began having a lot of chest pains. I took him to the emergency room and they did chest x-rays. The doctor on staff told me that his heart was enlarged. I freaked. The next day I took him to see his pediatrician. She told me that the radiologist report was normal. She did not know why the emergency room doctor had told me his heart was enlarged. She referred us out to a pediatric cardiologist at the children's hospital to have him checked out. We went for that appointment and they did another EKG. This EKG was abnormal. It showed something in the way his heart was beating. The cardiologist was concerned that either the walls of the heart were too thick or his heart was aged since they usually only see this pattern after a child has reached puberty. They took us straight in and did an ultrasound of his heart. This test was normal which showed no explanation for the strange rhythm.

I called Anthony's father who still lived on the east coast, crying. He said that he felt bad that he was not here going through this with us, but he would come as soon as he could. He told me I would never have to go through this kind of stuff with Anthony alone again. He got on the phone with Anthony and told him he would be here as soon as he could make the arrangements. The next few weeks he called Anthony on a daily basis, telling him how excited he was about coming back, and being able to be close to him and spend more time with him again. He had a job offer and was all set to leave there in one week. We were making plans for his return when I received an anonymous call exposing a girlfriend he had been involved in without my knowledge for the past year since I had left there. His girlfriend didn't want him to come back to California. She called me crying, telling me she loved him and didn't want to lose him and by the way, she was carrying his baby. Needless to say things changed and he never did come. I divorced Anthony's father for the second time.

The doctor decided to put Anthony on a heart monitor, which he had to wear 24 hours a day for 30 days. Boy was that fun! Anthony got a rash on the area that I had to place the patches. He complained constantly that it itched. Sometimes on the weekend if we were going to be home I didn't make him wear the monitor to try to give his skin a break. I always had it close by and could hook it up in a matter of seconds if I needed to. I had to place the patches on each side of his chest and then snap the wires on. Then they were plugged into a small box like a pager. He had to clip it to his pants. He was taught how to use the monitor. If he had any problems he had to push the button in the center. It would then go back and record 60 seconds prior and record for 60 additional seconds. It made a loud noise while it recorded. If he pushed the button accidentally, then he could pull out the cord from the box and stop the recording and it would reset. It was hard to keep it on him. Kids would mess with it when he was at school, and he would constantly pull on the cord, making the patches come off. After the first week the newness wore off and he got more used to it. We recorded a few episodes of chest pains. Then I had to call it in and send the record. In the full 30 days it never showed anything substantial. So we waited a couple of months. It seemed to go by with no problem. I signed him up for soccer. He got to play one game. Then he started having chest pains again. This time he lay around all weekend. He kept complaining that he didn't feel good and his chest was hurting. Sunday evening, he acted like he felt better and got up to play fetch with our dog. He ran around playing with the dog and in a matter of minutes he was doubled over with severe chest pains. I suggested we just try to go to bed and see how he felt. He still complained, so I got up and took him back to the emergency room. His heartbeat was irregular. It would beat fast, pause, beat slow, and then speed up again. They did another EKG. The emergency room doctor advised me there was nothing he could do to help except give Anthony something for the pain. He made a copy of the EKG so I could fax it to the cardiologist first thing the next morning. The next day, the cardiologist was not in. The following day, they called me and told me to bring him in right away; they wanted to put Anthony on the heart monitor again for 30 days. He wore the monitor for another 30 days and it was uneventful. As it stands at this point, several more months have passed with no problems. We are waiting to see if he has any more problems and we will address the situation at that point.

We went through some more behavioral therapy. Anthony still sometimes goes through phases of noncompliance. One thing I am thankful for is how he has learned to control himself. He has learned not to express his frustration with violence toward others or me. We even have a new dog, which he loves and helps care for. He is no longer mean to animals and loves to play with our dog, love on him, and pet him. Anthony is very attached to the dog and the dog loves Anthony. We only had a few short sessions to modify some of his behavior. We worked on helping him to be a little more independent and less attached to me. I began preparing him for a change. I told him that when he turned seven he would have to start sleeping in his own room. That was a goal I set for both of us. Although he had his own room for many months he still slept in his bed in my room. I told him this was the day and we took down the extra bed in my room. I hooked up a monitor in his room to reassure him that if he had any problem all he had to do was call. I had already started sitting on the side of the bed in my room and holding his hand until he fell asleep. He first had to be broke from the habit of twisting my hair to fall asleep. It was hard but he adjusted. When he moved into his room, I continued to do the same thing. I sat on the side of the bed and held his hand until he fell asleep. His sleep pattern is still different. The only time he sleeps through the night is if he goes to bed very late. Most nights at some point he ends up in my bed and I don't even know it until he pulls my hair by playing with it. He sometimes begs and almost cries to play with my hair but the answer is always no. He never has been one of those children that went to bed alone and went to sleep. He has never liked waking up in a room alone; he would be scared and cry. He no longer cries he just climbs into my bed. If I ever get married again this may be a problem we have to work on. My next goal is to get him to go to sleep in the room by himself, which is what we are working toward at this point.

Anthony had his first experience of dealing with the death of a loved one when my grandmother died a couple of years ago. We talked about dying and going to heaven. He did not want to go to the funeral, although he had many questions. A couple of days after she died he told me that he had a dream. He said great grandma was in heaven with his grandpa. She was happy and was swimming, which is one of his favorite things to do. My mother shared the dream with my relatives. My grandmother had never learned to swim while she was alive.

When Anthony was younger, he rode the handicap bus. He used to tell me that my father, who had died sometime before his conception, would ride the bus with him so he wouldn't be scared. He never knew my father but told me that my father loved to fish and this was the truth.

When Anthony was very small, we talked about his grandpa because he knew nothing about him. I asked, "Do you know where your grandpa is?" I was trying to figure out how to explain death to him. He looked at me and pointed to a picture of Jesus my mom had hanging on the wall and he said, "I know where he is, he's with him". We had never told him that this was a picture of Jesus, or where Jesus lived. He sometimes talks about the baby that was inside my tummy that died. He wanted to know if the baby was up in heaven with grandpa too. He sometimes cries about it and says I really wanted a baby brother.

On the inside Anthony is a very soft and gentle person. He cares what people think of him. It hurts his feelings when others say or do mean things to him. Almost every night when he is getting ready to fall asleep he will often share with me the things that happened in his day. He sometimes tells me things other kids say to make fun of him with little tears in his eyes. Most of all I think he desperately longs for the love and acceptance from his father. This can be heart breaking for the both of us at times. His father does visit him for a week a couple of times a year. Whenever it is time for him to leave, Anthony would be heart broken and beg his dad to stay. Anthony talks to him on the phone often. He tells his father how much he misses him, loves him, and he often begs his father to come home. When his father says he can't come right now but maybe someday, Anthony cries and sometimes I cry right along with him. I continually pray that God will help Anthony to get through this.

Anthony's successes and improvements have been a slow process, but we reap the benefits everyday. With every new day there are things he accomplishes that years ago I felt were only a dream for him. Anthony sometimes asks if he is different or if there is something wrong with him. I tell him that God made everyone different. Some people are crippled or blind, others may look different or act different, but God made him just the way he wanted him to be and God don't make junk. He laughs and says," Your silly mom". His behavior has improved so much. Other than becoming hyper at times, he is pretty well behaved. He now understands what behavior is expected of him and if I correct him, he often says, "I know Mom, I'm sorry". He loves going to church and making new friendships there. He sometimes still tries to tell me how to drive or which way to go and I remind him that I am the driver and when he is old enough to drive he can choose how he wants to drive or which way he wants to go. He still watches a new movie several times when he first gets it. Now when I tell him Ok this is the last time for that one, pick another one; he does so without any problem. He can now swing on a swing with no problem and enjoys swinging and jumping off.

Sometimes when I drop him off at school he will have a hard time getting out of the car if there is a crowd of kids waiting for the bus. I sometimes have to back up so that he can get out of the car where there are no children waiting. One day the wheel on his backpack was squeaking and he came back to the car. He told me he could not walk past the group of kids waiting for the bus with his backpack making that noise. He was concerned it would bother them or draw attention to him. I had to get out of the car and put the straps on his back and he was then able to walk past them.

He sometimes asks to take a cold lunch to school. One morning I was getting his lunch ready and he looked to see what I had put in it for him. He took the pudding cup out. I asked, "What are you doing?" He said, "I can't take that to school." He said, "I can eat that at home but I can't take that to school because the kids make fun of me because it says Jell-O not pudding." I said, "Okay how about if I put the pudding in a little bowl?" He said, "That would be great mom." We have to sometimes be inventive with ideas to work around problems or situations that are uncomfortable for him.

He is maintaining a healthy weight and is still on the slim fast diet plan. God has blessed us. We have worked through our problems with Gods help instead of using methods a lot of doctor's prescribe. Anthony has never been on any medication; I have never tried the vitamin and mineral supplement programs others have tried. I make the best choices I know how to make and God picks up the slack on everything else.

Anthony is no longer shy or withdrawn. In fact, just last month, we went to Las Vegas and we went to a dance show. A couple of the girls came down into the audience and picked some of the kids to go up on stage with them. One girl picked him and he went up on the stage and he danced with them in front of the audience. He was so proud of himself. Last weekend, my niece got married and he once again displayed his moves on the dance floor with a bunch of strangers. And once again, with tears of joy rolling down my face, I look to the heavens and thank you God for this wonderful gift.

Anthony is ending another season of baseball. God has been so wonderful to place awesome men in his life. This year his coach has been exceptional. He has taken Anthony under his wing and has truly brought out the best in him this season. He tells him that he is his number one player; he encourages him, and tells him I know you can do it. He hits the ball really hard, and most of the time he hits it into the outfield. His coach always pats him on the back or gives him a high five and Anthony lights up. I have seen the encouragement of this man build self-confidence in my son that I have never seen before.

Anthony went on his first real field trip. Their class went on a field trip to the Zoo about 45 miles from home. He rode on a big bus for the first time. We talked about the trip several times. I did not request the day off because I had just returned from a few days vacation. The night before, I really began to be concerned how he would do on the trip without me. I kept asking him, "Do you want me to go? I will call and get the time off if you need me to go." I was the one hanging onto him. I said, "You've never rode the big bus before and you never went someplace like this without me before." The next morning, I asked him the same thing again. "Are you sure you can do this? I can call into work and go with you if you need me to." He looked at me with a real serious look on his face. He says, "Mom, I will be fine, I am a big boy now, and you can go to work." I could hardly wait until he got home. He did it without me, and had a really good time. I let out a big sigh of relief.

Anthony's seventh birthday has come and gone. He is just a few weeks from completing the first grade. A few weeks ago I asked the school system to have him re-evaluated by a speech pathologist and an occupational therapist to see if he was grade level in speech and if he was still delayed in fine motor skills. I had a meeting with the school psychologist and the speech pathologist that tested him. After gathering all the information from his past school records they could hardly believe how much progress he has made. His tests were all normal concerning his fine motor skills. The speech pathologist did seven tests on him. He scored at least average but higher then average on most of the tests. We talked for a few moments and I shared some of the story of where we started and they couldn't believe it. They were so amazed. The school psychologist told me that I had been a true inspiration to her and I had given her hope for all the kids and families she worked with going through the same thing right now.

Anthony is a wonderful child. I often say that God gave him an extra special personality to compensate because he knew what he would have to go through in life. God is so awesome. I have a wonderful son and I feel everyday that I am so blessed that God entrusted his care into my hands. He has brought so much joy and happiness to my family and me. He loves to laugh and giggle. He loves to play pool with me. He always tries to sneak up on me and scare me. He will often sneak into the freezer and get a piece of ice to sneak up and put it on me. He loves to do silly things to me. One morning, I kept telling him to get up and get dressed and I left the room. When I came back he was still in the bed. I told him very firmly you need to get dressed or you are going to be late for school. He had the covers pulled up to his neck and was trying real hard not to laugh. I said, "What's so funny"? He threw the covers back and jumped out of the bed, he was completely dressed including his shoes. He was so happy that he had played a joke on me. Anthony loves a lot of attention. He loves to be tickled. To have him in my life everyday is a gift from God. He is truly a priceless Gift from God.

13

AND LIFE GOES ON

Around the time Anthony turned eight years old, we went back to the neurologist. The Neurologist did several tests, interviewed Anthony and me, and observed him for some time. This appointment took about two and a half hours. The doctor's findings were very interesting. Although Anthony still displayed a few autistic behaviors, some ADHD, and obsessive-compulsive behaviors, he no longer displayed enough behaviors to meet the criteria of carrying the diagnosis of autism any more. You can not imagine how I felt being told this. I had been praying, asking God for Anthony's healing for years. Now this doctor just confirmed just how far God had brought us and how much progress Anthony had actually made.

I talked to the neurologist about the area in which we lived. There is not a lot of support given to those children in need of services. Our county is very poor, one of the poorest in California, and made up of mostly migrant farm workers. The schools don't have the funds or the man power for special aids. The space available in special education classes is limited, and there is no special curriculum geared for kids with autism. I have asked every teacher that Anthony has had if any of them were required to take any teacher training on how to handle any special needs kids in a regular classroom. Every teacher answered the same. There was no formal education required or offered in the regular educational system to train teachers how to deal with issues that may arise having kids with special needs in there classroom. I seriously think that some sort of education should be mandatory for the teachers. The way the system works now, they try to mainstream kids with special needs into regular education classes as soon as possible, but yet do nothing to prepare the teacher to teach them and see to it that their needs are met. Who should be accountable for this? I have actually spent my time and effort trying to educate every one of his teachers about Autism and ADHD behaviors and symptoms. We recognize that our children are different, we try to adapt our home life to an environment that works for them, and then we send them to school for seven hours a day and entrust them to a teacher that has no training on how to teach them or to understand their differences from the other children. It is my opinion that all teachers in every state should be required to take some classes to learn how to educate those children with special needs. The doctor suggested that I consider moving to a different area or state.

In doing my research for this book I checked into the current regulations where I live. When I contacted the Board of Education, I was told they have no certain requirement as long as the teacher has a degree; it is up to the college to decide what classes are required to get a teaching degree. I have a niece that is currently in the process of getting a teaching degree. She is attending a California State University. She told me they are given a choice of four classes. It is up to each student to choose the class they want to take. The four classes are as follows:

Child and Family Crisis; which has do with child abuse, divorce, remarriage, death, substance abuse, disability, immigration, poverty. (In my opinion this class should be mandatory)

Psychological Aspects of Physical Disability; this class teaches theory and research pertaining to physical disabilities and the impact of the disability on an individual's behavior. It deals mainly with blindness, deafness, orthopedic handicap, epilepsy, cardiovascular disease, cancer and diabetes.

Understanding Special Populations in a Contemporary Society; basically understanding the terminology, etiology, legislation, facilities, trends and appreciation of similarities and differences.

Teaching Students with Special Needs in General Education Settings; introduction to identification, characteristics, theories, curriculum, and instruction for students with mild to severe disabilities, legislative guidelines, nondiscriminatory assessment, parental involvement and foundations in special education.

It is up to the student which of these four classes is chosen. Why isn't this class mandatory? In my opinion it should be. With the epidemic of autism and the large number of children diagnosed with ADHD each year, there is a 100% chance that a teacher will end up with special needs kids in their class at some point. My research was conducted on a college in California, other states requirements may be different, because it is up to the college to select the classes that are required to obtain a degree.

My older son had moved to Texas a few months before and really loved it. We checked into the schools and found that in Texas the teachers are required to have taken some special education classes. They were trained to handle kids with Autism and ADHD. It took some time but we moved out of our apartment and stayed with my mom for a few weeks and then moved. We both loved the area. We had a lot of fun exploring our new surroundings. Anthony played baseball again that season. Living in Texas was a whole different life then the life we had lived in California. The people were nicer and more helpful. While we were in Texas we did a lot of things we had never done before. We went to a live Mavericks basketball game; we went to several baseball games. Anthony really became more interested in sports and watching sports on TV. He likes to watch football and auto racing when ever he finds it on.

The schools in Texas were built totally different. All the classes and hall ways were inside the building. In California all of the halls and walk ways are open between classes and the cafeteria. In Texas the schools seemed so much safer since you had to go by the office and be buzzed in to enter any of the buildings. They had computer labs with several computers, enough for each student to use. The food was better with a lot more item choices and the cafeteria was a large open space in the middle of all the rooms. Anthony went to a separate room for music and art classes every day. He loved the school, his teacher and all the new friends he was making. He really seemed happy for the first time in a really long time. After the school year ended, he went to the Boys & Girls Club of America during the day while I worked. They made field trips weekly. He got to go to an Aquarium in the city of Ft Worth and he got to go bowling, (one of his favorite things to do). They made trips to the movies, arcades and fun centers. He had an awesome summer.

We got some news that my mom was having some heart problems. It was hard for us being so far away. Then one day my older son got a job offer back in California, so we all decided to move back. It amazes me how much Anthony has changed. Thankfully, now he adapts much more easily. We moved back and I went to work the next week. He started third grade in a whole new school, just down the street from my office.

Later that year, Anthony returned to the cardiologist. He still experiences a rapid heart rate and chest pains occasionally. We have learned that this usually happens when he is upset, or is under a lot of stress. The doctor explained that when Anthony is too excited or upset, he needs to calm down, take deep breaths, and slow down his breathing. This will help to slow down his heart rate and relieve the chest pain. These exercises have helped in calming him down and getting his heart rate to slow down the more he relaxes. We hope in time he will out grow this problem. Other than that his health is doing well.

Anthony has come so far and has made too many accomplishments to name them all. There are still days when he gets tired and things may be a little hard for him. There are times his reactions or actions in a given situation may be different from other children. I have learned that he processes information differently than I do.

Anthony's relationship with his father has deteriorated even more. On the last visitation some things took place that were very upsetting to both Anthony and I. Anthony has come to the point that he no longer wants his father to be a part of his life. He no longer talks to his father on the phone and has not seen him for over two years.

There are still some things he has difficulty understanding. He doesn't understand why people divorce, or how dads can abandon their own children. He doesn't know how someone can be your best friend and not choose you on their team when they want to play football or baseball. He doesn't understand why kids say mean things to other kids to hurt their feelings, or why grown ups yell when they are angry. He is very complex, with knowledge beyond his years.

Anthony is not perfect, but for the most part, he acts just like any other normal kid his age. Sometimes, I have to remind myself to be careful not to try to squeeze him into a "Normal" mold, by expecting normal behavior from him even when he is going through a tough time. He continues to excel. Sometimes there are some rough spots but for the most part our life is good.

Anthony's tenth birthday is coming up, he is maintaining A's and B's in fourth grade and has decided to not play baseball this season, four years in a row was enough for him. He loves riding his bike, scooter and begs for a dirt bike. In his spare time, he reads and plays video games and has finally mastered multiplication. He enjoys dancing to rap music, and displays some talent there; we plan to possibly start some hip hop classes soon. Whenever we are at a party where there is dancing going on, he is the center of attention, and can steal the dance floor with his moves. He is no longer shy or withdrawn. He has confidence and can go up to anyone and start a conversation. He can walk into a new class where he doesn't know anyone at school or church with no problem. He sleeps in his own room and goes to sleep in his own bed all alone. He talks of becoming a man and how hard it must be for a man to find the "perfect" woman.

One weekend, we went to visit a very close friend of mine. She ended up having to work on Saturday. She had arranged for Anthony, her children and I, to spend the day with her mother. I had not seen her mother in years although we had become friends many years before when her daughter and I had first met. She is a very sweet old woman and has been a Christian for many years. We spent the day talking about her book being published, talking about my book, and just spent the day with the kids and catching up. She had never met Anthony before, although she had helped to pray for him many times through the years. When she saw him, she said, "Come here, child". She held his chin, looked into his clear gray eyes for a long time, and then she told him to give her a hug. She looked at me and said, "Judy, this baby is no ordinary child, he is an angel kissed by God."

I know one thing for sure; I could never have endured these past ten years without God. God has proven to me that he is always true to his word.

*

Who forgives all your iniquities, Who heals all your diseases.

Psalms 103:3 (KJV)

*

When there were mountains, God removed them. When there were obstacles, God eliminated them. When there were valleys, we stopped and thanked God for his many blessings. When there were steep hills to climb, God gave us the strength and endurance to make it to the top. God was there the whole time working His plan. With Gods guidance and direction, He has brought us to the land of promise.

14

EDUCATION & TREATMENT

When you have a child that has just been diagnosed with Autism, it may seem as though you have been dropped into a whirlwind of information, choices, and decisions that need to be made. What treatments to try? What medication or dietary changes are needed? There are lengthy federal regulations that need to be read and understood, and articles filled with one view or another about the controversial issues concerning autism. Some of the decisions you will need to make may come from areas where you don't feel adequately informed. Of these important decisions, many will be in the area of education.

Educating children with autism is a challenge for both parents and teachers. These children are individuals first and foremost with unique strengths and weaknesses. Some may be average or above average in intelligence, while others may be below average. Academic goals need to be tailored to each individuals intellectual ability and functioning level.

Just as there are various treatment approaches, there are multiple educational programs that provide stimulating learning environments. The Individuals with Disabilities Education Act (IDEA) is a federal mandate that guarantees students with disabilities a free, appropriate public education.

The common thread in autism is the presence of a developmental disability, more specifically, a disorder of communication which manifests itself differently in each person. But whatever the level of impairment, the educational program for an individual with autism should be based on the unique needs of the student. If this is the first attempt by the parents and school system to develop an appropriate curriculum, conducting a comprehensive needs assessment is a good place to start. This evaluation will become the blueprint for your child's educational plan.

Educational planning for students with autism often address a wide range of skill development, including academics, communication and language skills, social skills, self—help skills, and behavior modification. It's important to consult with professionals trained specifically in autism to help the child benefit the most from his or her school program. If you are involved in support groups associated with autism, you may be able to get some much needed input and advice from parents who have already been through the process. Some parents have become real advocates for their children and don't mind attending school meetings with other parents as support and to give guidance. It is very important to get a wide range of opinions and to keep a close eye on your child's progress or lack thereof.

Most professionals agree that individuals with autism respond well to highly structured, specialized education programs designed to meet their individual needs. Based on the characteristics associated with autism, there are areas important to look at when creating a plan that will work for your child. **These are key issues to think about: social skill development, communication, behavior, and sensory integration.** Programs have to sometimes include several treatment components coordinated to assist a person with autism. For example, one individual's may consist of speech therapy and social skill development all within a structured behavior program. Another child's may include social skill development, sensory integration, and dietary changes. No one program or diet is perfect for every person with autism. It's important to try several approaches and find ones that work best for your child. I can't stress this enough; **get involved in a support group as soon as you can**.

The support from others helps you to stay focused and on track, rather than feeling overwhelmed and helpless. Talk to other parents and see what treatments worked best for their kids. Talk about your particular school district and see what issues others have faced with teachers and schools. It helps a lot to just talk to someone that has been going through the same things and thinking and feeling the same things you are right now. Trust the input and experience of what other parents tell you over the opinions of educators and others involved in the school district meetings. Don't be afraid to tell people your ideas and feelings about certain issues, after all it is your child. With all of that said, parents and professionals need to work together. Teachers need to have some understanding of the child's behavior and communication skills at home, and parents should let the teachers know their expectations as well as what techniques work at home. Open communication between the parents and the school staff can lead to a better assessment of your child's needs. Cooperation between parents and professionals can lead to increased success for the individual with autism.

Academic goals need to be tailored to the individuals intellectual ability and functioning level. Some children may need help in understanding social situations and developing appropriate responses. Others may exhibit aggressive or self-injurious behavior, and may need assistance managing their behaviors. No one program will meet all the needs of any individual with autism, so it is important to develop one that meets your child's individual needs. Just like with treatment approaches, educational programs need to be tailored to your child's individual needs and will need to be re-evaluated on a regular basis.

To understand your child's rights in America's public schools, it helps to start with one of the primary laws governing the education of children with disabilities: the Individuals with Disabilities Act, or IDEA. IDEA is a federal law that guarantees a free and appropriate public education for every child with a disability. This means that if you enroll your child in a public school, his or her education should be at no cost to you and should be appropriate for his or her age, ability and development level.

IDEA has both statutes and regulations. IDEA establishes the minimum requirements schools must provide. For states to receive federal funds, they must meet the eligibility funding criteria of IDEA. States may exceed the requirements and provide more services. They cannot, however, provide less nor have state regulations or practices that contradict the guidelines of IDEA.

The federal regulations do not require states to provide an "ideal" educational program or a program the parents may feel is "best." The state must provide an appropriate educational program, one that meets the needs of the individual student.

Parents need to be aware of the educational rights and the placement options available. There is not a "one size fits all" model for education of children with disabilities. Placement options range from total inclusive settings where children with autism receive their education alongside non-disabled peers to private placement in residential programs for children with disabilities.

Determining the most appropriate placement for your child is a two-step process:

1. Determine your child's level of function and associated needs by requesting an evaluation or re-evaluation through the school or an independent professional. This evaluation should include specific recommendations for supports, educational services and levels of treatments.
2. Develop a well-defined and thorough Individual Education Plan, in collaboration with your child's prospective teacher, service providers and school administrator. Discuss all the options that meet the needs of your child. How does the school currently provide services for children with disabilities? Are there programs currently in place that can be modified to meet your child's needs? Using this information, you and the school together can determine your child's placement.

The law begins with the assumption that, to the maximum extent possible, children with disabilities should be educated with their non-disabled peers. Once the child's needs are assessed and necessary services and supports are determined, the placement options should begin with the regular or inclusive classroom. Children with disabilities do not have to start in a more restrictive or separate class and then "earn" the right to move to a less restrictive placement. If it is found that a regular education classroom would not meet the child's needs, even with support services, then another option may need to be pursued. Keep in mind that the child with a disability must benefit from the placement.

The law specifies that education placement should be determined individually for each child, based on the child's specific needs, not solely on the diagnosis or category. A safe educational environment is important for all children. School safety concerns are addressed in IDEA.

The first step in obtaining special education services is for a child to be evaluated for services. The evaluation can be done when your child is first suspected of having a disability or when your child's level of functioning changes in one or more areas. There are two ways in which a child can be evaluated under the regulations of IDEA.

1. Any parent can request an evaluation by calling or writing the director of special education or the principal of your child's school. If you call, also put your requests in writing and keep a copy for your records. You should make this a part of your routine communication with anyone concerning your child's education. Follow-up all telephone calls with a letter summarizing the conversation. This way the other party has the opportunity to make any corrections to any misunderstood information, and you have a paper trail in case of a disagreement with the school district.
2. The school may also determine an evaluation is necessary. If so, they must have written permission from the parent before an evaluation can be conducted.

An evaluation needs to be conducted by a team or group of persons, which must include at least one teacher or other specialist with specific knowledge in the area of suspected disability. The law requires the child be assessed in all areas but not limited to the suspected disability, including but not limited to, health, vision, hearing, communication abilities, motor skills, and social and emotional status.

If parents disagree with the results of the evaluation, they may choose to obtain an independent evaluation at public or private expense. A list of professionals that meet the states requirements may be requested from your child's school or you can choose one on your own. If the professional chosen meets the criteria set up by the state, then the school must consider their evaluation in developing an IEP.

Parents may suggest professionals with knowledge of autism be present at the school for these evaluations. The school does not have to use the suggested professional, but may appreciate the assistance in finding a qualified person. As explained above, if the parents disagree with the school's evaluation, they have the right to acquire an independent evaluation. The evaluation should become the basis for writing the child's IEP. The IEP must be prepared and agreed upon before placement decisions are made. The placement may not be chosen first, then the IEP written to fit the placement decision.

The Individualized Education Plan (IEP) is a written document that outlines the plan for the child's education. As the name implies, the educational program should be tailored to the individual student to provide maximum educational benefit.

The IEP is the cornerstone for the education of a child with a disability. It should identify the services a child needs so that he or she may grow and learn during the school year. It is also a legal document that outlines:

1. The child's special education plan by defining the goals for that school year.
2. Services needed to help the child meet those goals.
3. A method of evaluating the student's progress.

The objectives, goals and selected services are not just a collection of ideas on how the school may educate a child. The school district must educate your child in accordance with the IEP.

To develop an IEP, the local education agency officials and others involved in the child's educational program meet to discuss education related goals. By law, the following people must attend the IEP meeting:

1. One or both parents.
2. The child's teacher or perspective teacher.
3. A representative of the public agency, other than the child's teacher, who is qualified to provide or supervise the provision of special education.
4. The child, if appropriate
5. Other individuals at the discretion of the parent or agency (such as a physician, advocate or neighbor).

The IEP is not complete until it had been thoroughly discussed and all parties agree to the written document. Parents are entitled to participate in the IEP meeting as equal participants with suggestions and opinions regarding their child's education. They may bring a list of suggested goal and objectives, as well as additional information that may be pertinent, to the IEP meeting. The local agency must attempt to schedule the IEP meeting at a time and place agreeable to both the school staff and parents. School districts are required to notify the parents in a timely manner so that they will have the opportunity to attend. The notice must explain the purpose of the meeting.

It is in everyone's best interest to remember that both parents and teachers share a common goal: to develop a program that will be appropriate for the child with autism. By sharing information and knowledge, parents and schools can collaborate to develop a truly effective IEP.

When preparing for your child's next IEP consider the following suggestions:

1. What is your vision for your child, for the future, and the next school year?
2. What are your child's strengths, needs, and interests?
3. What are your major concerns about his or her education?
4. In your child's education thus far, what has and has not worked?
5. Does the evaluation fit with what you know about your child?

While the IEP meeting is meant to develop an educational plan for your child, it is also an opportunity for you to share information about your child, your expectations, and what techniques have worked at home.

If a child already receives special education services the above standards apply for a re-evaluation as well. A re-evaluation must take place at least every three years. It may, however, be conducted more often if the parent or teacher makes a written request. A re-evaluation of all areas of suspected need or one for particular areas may occur if a parent feels their child is not meeting the short term objectives on the current IEP

Parents, who feel their child's placement should be changed, need to have a basis for this request. For example, a child may be exhibiting problem behaviors that were not previously exhibited. It may be necessary to reassess his placement or develop new behavior techniques to address this area. As a first step, an evaluation by a specialist familiar with autistic behaviors could be requested. The IEP can then be changed to reflect the results.

A re-evaluation of all area of suspected need may come prior to the scheduled annual IEP meeting. If a child has made significant progress since the last evaluation, the treatment, placement and therapy recommendations may not be applicable. A re-evaluation in all areas would become the basis for a more appropriate IEP.

An IEP should address all the areas in which a child needs educational assistance. This can include academic and non-academic goals, if the services provided will result in an educational benefit for the child. All areas of projected need such as social skills (playing with other children, responding to Q & A), functional skills (dressing, crossing the street to walk safely to the bus), related services (occupational therapy, speech therapy, physical therapy) can also be included in an IEP.

The IEP should list the setting in which the services will be provided and the professionals who will provide the service. The content of an IEP must include the following:

1. A statement of the child's present level of education performance. This should include both academic and non academic aspects of the child's performance.

2. A statement of annual goals that the student may reasonably accomplish in the next 12 months. This statement should also include a series of measurable, intermediate objectives for each goal. This will help both the parents and educators know whether the child is progressing and benefiting from his or her education. The development of specific, well defined goals and objectives is crucial to your child receiving an appropriate education.

3. Appropriate objective criteria, evaluation procedures and schedules for determining, at least annually, whether the child is achieving the short term objectives set out in the IEP. (For example," How we are judging whether intervention is successful?" "How long will my child be in this program?").

4. A description of all specific special education related services, including individualized instruction and related support services to be provided (e.g. occupational therapy, physical therapy, speech therapy, transportation, recreation). This includes the extent to which the child will participate in regular education programs.

5. The initiation date and duration of each service, as determined above, to be provided (this can include extended school year services). You may include the person who will be responsible for implementing each service.

6. If your child is 16 years old or older, the IEP must include a description of transitional services (coordinating set of activities designed to assist the student in movement from school to post school activities).

It is important that your child receives an appropriate education and therefore benefit from that education. Students with autism have the right to related services to help them learn and to receive the maximum benefit from their education program. Related services, according to IDEA, consist of "transportation and such developmental, corrective and other supportive services as are required to assist a child with a disability to benefit from special education." These services are to be determined on an individual need basis, not by the disability or the category of the disability.

If a child needs any of these "related services" to benefit from his or her education, they must be written into the IEP. Frequency and duration of services, as well as relevant objectives, should be included. Related services as defined by IDEA may include, but are not limited to the following:

1. Audiology
2. Counseling services
3. Early identification and assessment of disability in children
4. Medical services (for diagnostic or evaluation purposes only)
5. Occupational services
6. Parent counseling and training
7. Physical therapy
8. Psychological services
9. Recreation
10. Rehabilitation counseling
11. School health services
12. Social work services
13. Speech pathology
14. Transportation.

The regulation does not limit related services to those specifically mentioned above. If a child requires a particular service to benefit from special education and that service is developmental, corrective or supportive, it is also a "related service" and should be provided. It does not have to be specifically listed in the regulation. Examples of these kinds of services may include a full or part-time aid or assisted technology, such as a computer.

While the IEP goal and objectives should be child-centered, the document may also include information regarding teacher or staff training. If the IEP team decided that additional training is required for the student's teacher, this information must be included in the text of the IEP. For example, the team may decide it will be beneficial for a teacher to take an autism course at a local university. Or it may want the school support staff to attend a two-hour seminar on autism. Personnel standards and teacher certification requirements are established by each state. For more information on the state certification requirements in your area, please contact the appropriate state education agency.

Facing the decisions that need to be made by any parent going through this situation is not easy. There will be times when wrong choices are made and you will have to advocate for your child to get the services changed or increased. In my experience, with the school system in my area, you had to really push to get any services at all. My son was first evaluated through the Regional Center. Once he was given a diagnosis, the person that our case was assigned to regarding special education then contacted me. He was assigned to a special education class, but the only other service the school district provided was bus transportation. Once he was re-evaluated and put into a normal preschool setting transportation was stopped.

The regional center provided a behaviorist to come into our home and work with us. This process took a couple of months. First the person came to our home for an evaluation, then he made a treatment plan and it was submitted to the regional center for approval. It took several more weeks to get the actual therapy started. So don't be under the assumption that the help will come as soon as you ask for it. It can take several months to get all the services started.

The Regional Center also paid for respite services, so I was able to hire a person to come in and take care of Anthony for a few hours a month, to give me a break. Regional Center also reimbursed me for cost of Anthony's diapers.

Anthony had private insurance and we were required to use his insurance to pay for his speech therapy, occupational and sensory therapies. None of these services were added to his IEP. His IEP was for his special education class and bus transportation only; no other services were provided for him or paid for by the school district. If we had not had private insurance I am not sure what services they would have provided for him. It is very important that you educate yourself. The more you know the better equipped you will be to fight for your child's rights. If you don't know what is required or what services are available to you, no one will offer that information to you. You need to do your own research. Even though there are a lot of services that you can request, getting your regional center case manager or the school to implement those services can be difficult to accomplish. You will need to write letters, make phone calls, and be diligent to get the services you want for your child. The school system and the regional center funds are limited and they try their hardest not to give you the services even though you may think that your child may benefit from many of them. At least, that is the way it is where I live. Check into all the services available in your area. If there is something you want for your child then don't give up or back down until you get it.

Within the law, there are specific procedural safeguards to protect your child's rights. If you and the school disagree on the placement, educational program or about the services that will be provided, you may want to utilize one of the following approaches:

1. Discussion or conference with school staff. Staff may include the teachers, counselors or principal.
2. An IEP review. You may request an IEP review at any time.
3. Negotiation or mediation. Mediation is a voluntary process as described in IDEA in which a neutral third person assists the parties to work together to resolve their dispute. All states are required to have a mediation process established that meets the requirements of IDEA, including maintaining a list of qualified mediators and bearing the cost of the mediation process. Neither party is required to use mediation. The mediator cannot force either party to accept a resolution to the dispute. If a mutual satisfactory agreement is reached on some or all the issues, a written agreement is set forth. Discussions that occur during mediation are considered confidential and may not be used as evidence in subsequent proceeding.
4. Mediation must be available as a dispute resolution, but may not be used to deny or delay the right to a due process hearing.
5. Due process hearing. You may request a due process hearing if you do not agree with your child's identification, evaluation, or educational placement. This is a legal proceeding and you should obtain legal advice.

6. Complaint resolution procedures. Any individual or organization may file a complaint alleging that the local education agency has violated a requirement of IDEA. The complaint must be written and signed; it must site the specific IDEA requirement that was violated and the facts upon which the allegation is made. The state education agency must resolve the issues of the complaint within 60 calendar days after it is filed.

Once the team has come to an agreement and an IEP has been written, ongoing communication between the school and the parent is essential to the child's success. The IEP is a working document that can change over time and as progress is made. It should represent a program flexible enough to respond the changing needs and skills of the person with autism. The IEP team can meet at any time to discuss changes or additions that need to be made to the child's plan at any time.

Many parents seek out assistance from the education advocates or disability advocates. To help you better understand your child's rights under federal law, and more effectively communicate with professionals regarding your child's education, each state has a federal funded Parent Training Information Center or PTI that provides information and assistance to parents facing the educational process. PTI's are designed to teach parents basic advocacy techniques and encourage parents to become full participants in their child's education.

Every state also has a Protection and Advocacy Agency. Originally these agencies were set up to protect individuals with disabilities from abuse and neglect; however, their scope is much broader now. In many of the agencies, their advocacy centers around helping families obtain free, appropriate, public education for their children. State Protection and Advocacy Agencies offer training, case management, and legal counseling in many instances.

The U.S. Department of Education's Office of Special Education Programs (OSEP) can also be a resource of information on education rights. If you have a question regarding IDEA and can't seem to get an answer in your state, you may write to OSEP for clarification of the law, Contact OSEP directly at the Office of Special Education Programs, U.S. Department of Education, 400 Maryland Avenue SW, Mail Stop 2651, Washington DC, 20202, 202-205-5507.

15

FACTS ABOUT AUTISM

In January 2003, a report was issued from the Center for the Study of Autism. According to these figures, the California Department of Developmental Services or DDS, experienced an astounding 31% one-year increase in the number of new children professionally diagnosed with the most severe cases of Autism entering its Developmental Services System. In California alone, the 31% one-year increase from 2001 to 2002 represented an all time record number of new cases in the system's 33-year history. The golden state, however, is said to operate the golden standard of autism epidemiology, having always tracked "full-blown" autism only, defined by the DSM-IV manual. In other words, children with milder forms of the disorder such as persons with PDD-NOS, Aspergers, or any other spectrum disorders are not counted, just those who have received a professional diagnosis of Autism.

According to the Department, eight years before, in 1994, there were 5,108 cases of Autism in the entire system. As of January 6, 2003, there were now 20,377 cases of Autism. Since 1980, the documented start of California's Autism epidemic, the number of new cases has exploded. In 2003, California was adding, on average, 10 new children a day, seven days a week with the most severe form of Autism into its system, an increase of 2 children over the 2001 rate. To put in perspective, from January 1994 to January 1995, California added an average of two new children a day; and now we are adding 10. In 2006, Autism now accounts for 47 % of all the new intakes into the system, making Autism the number one disability entering California's DDS.

California's rate of increase is at epidemic proportions. During the school year of 2000 to 2001 there were 3,422 cases of Autism reported in California's school system, 2,244 in New York, and 1,108 cases reported for Texas. All other states reported in the hundreds or less.

In 2005 there were 28,046 persons with Autism in California's system compared to 13,054 in 2000, an increase of 14,992 children in 5 short years. It took over 32 years from 1969 to April 2001 to add a total of 14,777 new children to the entire system; it took just five years, from July 2000 to July 2004 to add 14,992 new children. In effect, the new caseload growth in those five years surpassed the ENTIRE caseload growth for the first 32 years of the systems history!

Over 80% of California's 31,853 persons with full syndrome autism are between the ages of three and seventeen years of age, meaning only 2 out of every 10 persons affected by this disorder are over the age of eighteen. There are more fourteen year olds than fifteen year olds, and more thirteen year olds than fourteen year olds, and so on. A total of 88% of the autism population currently lives at home.

It is important to note, that in California's Developmental Service System, children under the age of three years old are not counted in the DDS's quarterly reports. DDS reports that nearly 90% of all persons with autism in California's system entered the system between the age of three and six years old.

In 2002, California's all time record year for the number of new cases of professionally diagnosed, full syndrome, DSM IV autism, entering it's developmental services system with 3,577 new cases. The calendar year 2003 marked the first decline in new cases since California began tracking this mysterious disorder. In calendar year 2003 the number of new cases dropped to 3,125 new cases and in calendar year 2004 the number of new cases dropped again to only 3,074. California has added 1,470 new cases compared to 1,518 cases for the same time period in 2004. A similar downward trend of newly reported cases has declined in Indiana too, and other states numbers should be available soon. According to the data just recently released during the third quarter of 2006, California added 841 new cases of Autism into its system. Although this number represents the second highest quarterly reported number of new cases in the systems 37 year history. The most recent numbers indicate that during the most recent 45 month reporting period from January 2003 through September 2006 there has been a 50% increase in the autism caseload. The rate has declined by nearly half over the previous like reporting period. The rate of increase has slowed by close to half from 97% to 50% during the past 45 months. Even though we are beginning to see a downward trend of new cases during some quarters reported, the autism epidemic is still very real.

*

Q: Autism, what is it?
A: Autism is not a disease, but a developmental disorder of brain function. Autism is a type of pervasive developmental disorder. It interferes with a person's ability to communicate with and relate to others. Autism is a lifelong condition that results in some degree of social isolation.

*

Q: What is Pervasive Developmental Disorder, or PDD-NOS (Pervasive Developmental Disorder—Not otherwise Specified?
A: PDD-NOS is a diagnosis by exclusion. When comparing PDD-NOS to Autism, PDD-NOS is used as a diagnosis when a child has symptoms of Autism, but not in the configuration needed for an Autism diagnosis. In a child that has Autism, a social component is where the most impairment is seen. Children who fail to meet the criteria for Autism and don't have adequate social impairment typically have a developmental disability, but not Autism. The term PDD is used as being the same as Autism Spectrum Disorders, which include, Autistic Disorder, Asperger's Disorder, Rett's Disorder or Childhood Disintegrative Disorder. NOS or not otherwise specified means the symptoms of the child do not specifically fit into any one of these categories. The child may show characteristics of many things like Autism Spectrum, ADD, ADHD, or OCD. The child may demonstrate some spectrum behaviors but not enough to pinpoint any one disorder, because the symptoms do not fit diagnostically into one category. If this is the case a Professional might decide that a diagnosis of PDD-NOS is warranted. A diagnosis of PDD-NOS is not necessarily a less severe one than a diagnosis of Autism, but can be sometimes.

*

Q: What are the symptoms of Autism?
A: People with classic Autism show three types of symptoms: impaired social interaction, problems with verbal and nonverbal communication, and unusual or severe limited activities and interests. Symptoms of autism usually appear during their first three years of childhood and continue throughout life.

*

Q: How will Autism affect my child?
A: Autism affects how a person perceives and processes sensory information. Signs of Autism almost always develop before a child is 3 years old, although the condition is frequently not diagnosed until later. Typically, parents first become concerned when they notice their toddler does not respond or interact like other children of the same age.

*

Q: What are some signs I can look for?
A: Children with Autism do not usually babble or talk normally, and they may seem to have hearing problems. Children with Autism may fail to respond to their names and often avoid looking at other people. They often have difficulty interpreting the tone of voice or facial expressions and do not respond to others' emotions or watch other people for cues about appropriate behavior. They appear unaware of others' feelings toward them or of the negative impact their behavior has on other people. Many children with Autism engage in repetitive movements such as rocking and hair twirling, or in self-injurious behavior such as biting or head banging. They also tend to start speaking later than other children and may refer to themselves by name instead of "I" or "me". Some speak in a sing-song voice about a narrow range of favorite topics, with little regard for the interest of the person to whom they're speaking. People with autism often have abnormal responses to sounds, touch, or other sensory stimulation. Many show reduced

sensitivity to pain. They also may be extraordinarily sensitive to other sensations. These unusual sensitivities may contribute to behavior symptoms such as resistance to being cuddled. All people with autism have difficulty with social interactions and relationships. Parents often describe their child with Autism as preferring to play alone and making little eye contact with other people. Other symptoms of Autism include difficulties with verbal and nonverbal communication, delayed language development, limited, repetitive and overused patterns of behavior, interest, and play. Many typical behaviors such as repetitive body rocking, unusual attachments to objects, and holding fast to routines and rituals, are driven by the need for sameness and resistance to change. There is no standard or typical person with Autism. Although Autism is defined by the above characteristics, people with autism can have many different combinations of behaviors in mild to severe forms.

*

Q: Who is affected most by Autism?
A: Autism strikes males about four times as often as females, and has been found throughout the world in people of all racial and socioeconomic backgrounds.

*

Q: Are there different severities of Autism?
A: Autism varies a great deal in severity. The most severe cases are marked by extremely repetitive, unusual, self-injurious, and aggressive behavior. This behavior may persist over time and prove very difficult to change, posing a tremendous challenge to those who must live with, treat, and teach these individuals. The mildest form of Autism resembles a personality disorder associated with a perceived learning disability. Some individuals need assistance in almost all aspects of their daily lives, while others are able to function at a very high level and can even attend school in a regular classroom.

*

Q: What research has been done to learn more about the cause of Autism?

A: Most researchers suggest that people with Autism have irregular brain structures. More study is needed to determine the cause of these irregularities, but current research indicates that they are inherited. Autism has no single cause. Researchers have identified a number of genes that play a role in the disorder. In some children, environmental factors also may play a role in development of the disorder. Studies of some people with Autism have found abnormalities in several regions of the brain. These abnormalities suggest that Autism results from the disruption of normal brain development early in fetal development. Scientists estimate that, in families with one Autistic child, the risk of having a second child with the disorder is approximately 5%, or one in 20. Most researchers are looking for clues about which genes contribute to this increased susceptibility. In some cases, parents and other relatives of an Autistic person show mild social, communicative, or repetitive behavior that allow them to function normally but appeared linked to Autism.

*

Q: How do we get a diagnosis?

A: If you were concerned that your child has many of these symptoms, or demonstrates these types of behaviors, my suggestion would be to observe your child over a few weeks. Make notes, chart, or journal the types of behavior, the duration and how often the behaviors are demonstrated. If the behaviors have been consistent over several weeks, contact your child's pediatrician or family doctor.

Make an appointment to have your child evaluated by a Health Care Professional. Take the journal or material you have charted with you to your appointment and discuss your concerns with the doctor. Your Health Care Professional will evaluate a child suspected of having autism or another developmental delay using the diagnostic guidelines established by the American Academy of Child and Adolescent Psychiatric. A child may also have hearing and other tests to make sure developmental delays aren't the result of another condition with similar symptoms. It should be up to your doctor to make an assessment of your child and then proceed with whatever tests are necessary to reach a diagnosis.

*

Q: What criteria are used to make a diagnosis?

A: This criterion is generally used to evaluate a child for Autism who does not interact with or socialize normally for his or her age. Researchers and therapists have developed several sets of diagnostic criteria for Autism.

Some frequently used criteria include:

- Absence or impairment of imaginative and social play.
- Impaired ability to make friends with peers.
- Impaired ability to initiate or sustained a conversation with others.
- Stereotyped, repetitive, or unusual use of language.
- Restricted patterns of interest that is abnormal in intensity or focus.
- Apparent inflexibility to specific routines or rituals.
- Preoccupation with parts of objects.

Children with some symptoms of Autism but not enough to be diagnosed with the classic form of the disorder are often diagnosed with pervasive developmental disorder, not otherwise specified or PDD NOS.

In order for a diagnosis of Autism to be made, the person still needs to evidence problems in three broad areas:

- Social interaction
- Communication
- Stereotyped patterns of behavior.

However, the numbers of symptoms, which fall under these three broad areas, have been reduced from 16 to 12 to make the diagnosis easier.

The individual needs to demonstrate six symptoms spanning the three broad areas with at least two symptoms indicating social interaction deficits, and one symptom in each of the communication and stereotyped patterns of behavior categories.

The symptoms of which fall under the social interaction categories are:

- Marked impairment in the use of multiple nonverbal behaviors.
- Failure to develop age appropriate peer relationships.
- Lack of spontaneous seeking to share interest and achievements with others.
- Lack of social or emotional reciprocity.

The symptoms, which fall under the communication category, are:

- Delay in or lack of spoken language development.
- Marked impairment in conversational skills.
- Stereotyped or repetitive use of language.
- Lack of spontaneous age appropriate make-believe play or social imitative play.

The symptoms, which fall under the stereotyped patterns of behavior category, are:

- Preoccupation with at least one stereotype or restricted pattern of interest to an abnormal degree.
- Inflexibility to routines or rituals.
- Stereotyped and repetitive motor mannerisms.
- Preoccupation with parts of objects.

Besides at least six of these symptoms, there also needs to be delays in social interaction, social communication, or symbolic or imaginative play.

*

Q: Is there a cure for Autism?
A: There is no cure for autism at this present time.

*

Q: What treatment plans and Resources are available to me?

A: Therapies, or interventions, are designed to remedy specific symptoms in each individual. Behavior training, specialized therapy, parent education and support, and sometimes medications can often improve an Autistic child's problem behaviors, communication skills, and socialization. A child with Autism responds best to a highly structured, specialized education program tailored to his or her individual needs. However, specific treatment varies depending on the range of the individual's symptoms, which can contribute in many different ways and change overtime. Parents, school staff, and health professionals are usually all involved in planning a child's treatment. Early diagnosis and treatment helps young children with Autism develop to their fullest potential.

Again, if you feel your child falls into these categories mentioned, or they show signs listed, contact your local Health Care Professional as soon as possible. Please note that these symptoms listed should not be used as a diagnosis, this can only be done by a Health Care professional.

If you do not know Christ as your personal savior, I invite you to make a commitment today.

Pray the following prayer:

Father,
   I ask you to come into my heart and life. Fill my heart and mind with peace. I believe and confess with my mouth that Jesus Christ is your son, and the savior of the world. I believe that he died on the cross for all the sins of mankind including mine. I believe in my heart that you raised him from the dead.
   I ask you to forgive my sins. Lord, help me in my time of struggle and great need. I believe that your word says that by your stripes we are healed. I am claiming complete healing for my child today. Thank you lord for receiving me into your kingdom; I am now a child of God.
   These things I ask in the wonderful name of Jesus,
                           Amen

   You have made the first step. Contact a church organization or pastor near you and let him know that you have just dedicated your heart and life to God and you need to get connected with a church.

                              *

                              *

ADDITIONAL INFORMATION

*

*

The following books may be helpful in educating yourself further:

FACING AUTISM: GIVING PARENTS REASON FOR HOPE AND
GUIDANCE FOR HELP
BY: LYNN M. HAMILTON

BEHAVIOR INTERVENTION FOR YOUNG CHILDREN
WITH AUTISM:
A MANUAL FOR PARENTS AND PROFESSIONALS
BY CATHERINE MAURICE

WEB SITES WITH VALUABLE INFORMATION:

www.wrightslaw.com
www.tacanow.com
www.autism.org
www.autism-society.org
www.dds.cahwnet.gov